PSYCHOLOGY

GOES TO

WORK

PSYCHOLOGY
GOES TO
WORK

DR SANDI MANN

PURPLE HOUSE

Purple House Limited
75 Banbury Road
Oxford
OX2 6PE

© Sandi Mann 1998

Cover illustration © Franklin Hammond 1998

ISBN 1-84118-000-9

Printed in Great Britain by the Bath Press.

Cover design by Franks and Franks.

This book is dedicated to Dr Bernard and Mrs Rita Wilkins on the occasion of their Diamond Wedding Anniversary.

Contents

Contents

Acknowledgements

I would like to thank all those people who have contributed to this book by providing me with case studies, real-life examples and quotes. These are people who have allowed me access to their minds and thoughts in the course of my research. Similarly, I wish to convey my gratitude to those psychologists and researchers who have developed the theories and expertise that benefit workers today, and who have thus contributed to this text.

Special thanks must go to my publisher at Purple House, **Will Gompertz**, for all the encouragement, energy, support and humour that have kept me going throughout each stage of this manuscript preparation. Thanks also to **Victoria Warner** at Purple House for her skilled editing, and to **Liz Brown** for 'discovering' me after one of my media appearances.

I wish to acknowledge the practical help and emotional support of my partner, **Jonny Wineberg**, who has taken over most of my domestic and other arrangements in order to free my time to write this manuscript. His quiet (and successful) attempts at making my life easier have been a major factor in my writing and completing this book to a tight deadline.

Finally, thanks must go to my parents, **Pat** and **Martin Mann** for their interest in my life and work and for their frequent international faxes!

Introduction

Not so long ago, nobody needed a book called *Psychology Goes to Work*.

Workers generally stayed in the same job all their lives, worked nine to five, reached their sixties, received a carriage clock, and left; secure in the knowledge that they had done their job well.

No need then to understand how their boss's mind worked, or what made their colleagues tick. No need to do anything other, in fact, than your job: turn up, work, go home; move slowly and surely up the career path.

Since then, times have changed. A number of factors have resulted in a huge change of philosophy for today's worker who wants to reach the carriage clock stage.

First came the age of computer-chip technology, and with it came mass unemployment as bankers to production-line workers were replaced by machines. The growth of technology since then has been so rapid that the 'shelf life' of products and services is much shorter than it used to be: companies must now keep up with ever-changing technology just to survive, and failure to do so means more redundancies. Workers themselves must be receptive and adaptable to all these technological changes, and willing to adapt to the new patterns of working that such technology has brought with it: teleworking, freelancing, and so on.

The global marketplace has also changed: inflation and a strong Western economy means that countries can obtain cheaper goods from Asian or Third World markets. Mass import shrinks the manufacturing sector and the domestic workforce has found itself facing more unemployment.

Nor has the service sector been unaffected: over the last 10 or 20 years, the marketplace has been swamped with a proliferation of companies offering similar services and products. As a result, intense competition has led to downsizing, restructuring, merging, business process re-engineering and delayering over the economy as a whole. Such processes have created a new climate characterised by more unemployment, higher job insecurity and increased competition for fewer jobs.

With skilled labour overtaking unskilled, as technology infiltrates all areas of life, everybody is aware of the need for education and qualifications. Over the last 40 years, more people than ever have attended university. At work, quality management principles have seeped through from products to people, as different qualifications are now used to 'benchmark' workers. In other words, each and every worker competes with others who have equally strong qualifications or measures of success. A degree in your pocket is no longer sufficient to make you stand out from the crowd.

If qualifications, ability and talent are no longer enough to ensure progress in the new corporate jungle, what is?

This is where *Psychology Goes to Work*. What is needed now more than ever before is an empathy, an understanding and a special insight into the psychological factors of the work environment. Factors which include how to promote yourself without ingratiating yourself; how to read the rules of the organisational culture; how to fit into a team but also how to work on your own; how to assert yourself without appearing aggressive; how to lead and manage; how to cope with difficult people... All requirements which demand more psychological insight than written qualifications, more sensitive awareness than work ability, and more 'people' skill than 'product' skill.

Within the brave new world of the twentieth-century workplace, reaching a greater understanding of the working environment is the way forward. With this in mind, *Psychology Goes to Work* is filled with practical guidelines – based on psychological research, theory and insight – which will give you the competitive edge so badly needed in today's working world.

How Psychology Can Help

What is Psychology?

Psychology is the scientific study of mind and behaviour. It is scientific because psychologists develop and test theories to explain human behaviour in a scientific manner: in other words, under carefully-controlled conditions, its findings are subject to as much rigorous testing and re-testing as any other scientific experiment.

Psychologists typically divide their studies into four main disciplines: the biological, or physical, basis of mind and behaviour (how the brain, nervous system, hormones, and so on influence our thoughts and actions); the social basis of mind and behaviour (how other people, groups and relationships affect the way we think and act); the developmental basis (how our childhood and early development influence how we behave as adults); and the individual approach (how the inherent or inborn aspects of our personality or intelligence make us who we are).

What is Organisational Psychology?

It has long been recognised that the applications of psychology in business organisations are wide-ranging and varied. For example, research into the area of individual differences has led to the development of personality and intelligence tests, now used by many companies to help select candidates for jobs. Studies into the characteristics of a good leader can help psychologists train potential managers in management skills. A psychological understanding of the human reaction to change can help organisations going through mergers suffer the minimum amount of casualities in terms of people leaving their jobs, or having their work output reduced. Psychologists can help workers adapt to new technology, reduce stress, increase motivation, and build teams.

Unfortunately, such research is rarely made directly available to the workers themselves. The nature of academia is such that the majority of academic writings are unintelligible to non-psychologists, and it is therefore hard for non-psychologists to gain access to the valuable ways in which psychology can help them. Until now.

Psychology Goes to Work reveals how psychology works in the office, and gets it working: enabling you to work harder, and work smarter.

The Book

The primary aim of this book is to provide the reader with a unique insight into the psychological processes that occur in the work environment, and to provide the skills to make psychology work for the reader. By the end of this book, you should know exactly what is needed to give you a competitive edge in the new-millennial workplace. At the same time, you will be able to understand and use to your advantage the hidden codes at work, including non-verbal communication and office etiquette conventions, while getting on well with your colleagues, subordinates, seniors and clients. Your use of Impression Management, politics and networking will help you get ahead, while newly-gained psychological insights will make it easier to cope with the common workplace problems of stress, difficult colleagues or any career setbacks.

The Contents

Psychology Goes to Work contains case studies, examples, step-by-step plans and self-assessment quizzes. Having absorbed certain information and put it into practice, you can go back to the quizzes and re-assess yourself to see if your attitudes have changed.

The Chapters

Chapter 1: First Impressions Last: Personal PR and Impression Management

Impression Management is a skill that matters from the very first day. As first impressions are not easily overcome, it is important that you create, and maintain, a suitable image of yourself at work.

Do note: such behaviour is not Machiavellian or deceptive, it merely involves presenting your skills and attributes in an appropriate way. This chapter shows you:

1. How to communicate the appropriate message through dress, appearance and the appropriate body language.

2. How to be a professional at all times.

3. How to demonstrate enthusiasm.

4. How to practise mild ingratiation.

5. How to employ self-handicapping techniques.

Chapter 2: The Rules: Understanding Your Work Environment

Learning the rules which govern your organisation will make you acceptable, respectable, and promotable. Not all codes are formal or obscure: many are informal, and hidden, but it is absolutely crucial that you know what these are before you can truly succeed at work. You will learn:

Chapter 3: From the MD to the Canteen Staff: Getting on with Everyone at Work

Getting on with people is so much easier when you know what makes them tick. This chapter shows you how to get on with everyone who plays a part in your working life:

Chapter 4: In It Together: the Art of Teamwork

Having been integrated into your new post, you are likely to become a team or group member. Group pressures can exist in many forms: being aware of them will help you to function better within your team, and help your team to function better as a whole. In order to do this, an understanding of the following is required:

Chapter 5: The Office Grapevine: Gossip, Politics and Power at Work

Used appropriately and judiciously, gossip, politics and power can be essential and valuable contributors to your success. Each area, however, has its potential hazards as well as its advantages, and it is wise to be aware of – and thus profit from – the following:

3. The sexual politics minefield.

4. The gossiping minefield.

5. What to do when you tread on a 'mine'.

Chapter 6: Getting the Message: Communication at Work

Communication is implicit in almost everything we do, but rarely given the focus it deserves as a vital part of office life. Many large companies have communications departments or employees, as if these staff were the only ones who should or can do it. In reality, it infuses every part of everybody's working life. It is crucial that you know how to communicate effectively:

1. By telephone.

2. By email.

3. By letter, fax or memo.

4. In a meeting.

5. In a presentation.

6. Using body language.

Chapter 7: Take It Easy: Coping with Stress at Work

Stress and stress-related illnesses cost industry dearly, in terms of both absenteeism and lost productivity. The stressed worker also pays in terms of their mental and physical health.

The long and arduous climb to the top can only really be achieved (or at least sustained) by a worker who is healthy in mind, spirit and body: learning to cope with stress will benefit both you and your organisation. To cope successfully with stress, you should:

1. Understand what stress is and why it happens.

2. Identify how stressed you are.

3. Realise what the possible causes of your stress are.

4. Find methods for dealing with your stress and its causes.

5. Establish ways of dealing with your emotions at work.

6. Understand the link between personality and stress.

Chapter 8: Fight for Your Rights: Learning to be Assertive at Work

Those who are not assertive are often unable to voice opinions; are treated badly by colleagues; taken advantage of by the boss; passed over for promotion; unable to make requests; unable to give or receive compliments or complaints; and generally unable to progress into the more responsible and demanding job roles of which they are capable.

Being assertive (but not aggressive) will help you gain respect, credibility and professionalism. It involves:

1. Knowing how assertive you are.

2. Knowing the difference between assertion, aggression and passivity.

3. Boosting your self-esteem.

4. Understanding your rights.

5. Using assertiveness techniques.

6. Undergoing the big test of assertion: asking for a pay-rise or promotion.

Chapter 9: Onwards and Upwards: Climbing the Career Ladder
The final part of *Psychology Goes to Work* pays attention to some of the skills that are specifically needed for career advancement. These include:

1. Planning your career and career strategy.

2. Knowing how to deal with change.

3. Understanding the techniques of leadership.

Using the Book

It is intended that *Psychology Goes to Work* is used as a kind of worker's bible, guiding the employee along the path towards career success.

It is advised that you study the entire book initially, then keep it for reference when:

• relevant problems crop up at work.

• you start a new job or move to a different department with new rules, new people and new ways of working.

• the organisation is going through dramatic changes, like a merger.

• you encounter a new and unfamiliar situation at work.

• you are particularly stressed.

Armed with new insight and understanding, *Psychology Goes to Work* will accompany you into the workplace of the new millennium and equip you with all the necessary techniques for getting in, getting on and getting ahead.

For career advancement, read on.

Chapter One

First Impressions Last

The Aim

Career advancement – by creating and maintaining the right image at work.

"One of the most important lessons that I learnt from my first job is that the impression you create of yourself is everything. Why don't they teach you that at school?"

Clare, Account Manager

The reality of work as we head into the twenty-first century is that few tools in your box of work skills are more important than Personal PR and Impression Management. It took Clare two years to discover this secret behind workplace success: you will know it by the end of this chapter.

The employee who really wants to get ahead at work should engage continually in both Personal PR and Impression Managing activities. In today's climate of job insecurity, downsizing, restructuring, business process re-engineering, and the other buzzwords that describe the shrinking job market, doing your job well does not automatically guarantee you promotion. These days, creating a positive image in the workplace is the key to getting on at work.

Before your Impression Management skills can be developed, it is important to understand exactly what Impression Management is. Once you know that, you can tackle the first stage: your appearance. It is vital that you wear the right clothes, present yourself in a correct manner, and use the most appropriate body language.

It is not enough, however, to be perfectly groomed: you must also learn how to be a professional. At the same time, demonstrating an enjoyment of your job is also important, and you should learn how best to display your enthusiasm.

Ingratiation is a much under-estimated and maligned part of Impression Management; it is important to learn how this element of getting on with people can aid your progress in the workplace.

Another little-known area involves the art of self-handicapping: how to provide viable reasons for any mistakes you have made or your inability to finish a particular project.

Occasionally, of course, things go wrong and you need to know how to rescue, and when to rescue, any inadvertently bad impression you may have made.

Read on for your guide to successful Impression Management.

1. 'Personal PR' and 'Impression Management': What They Are, What They Aren't

W. H. Auden once said, 'The image of myself which I try to create in my own mind in order that I may love myself is very different from the image which I try to create in the mind of others in order that they may love me'. [Source: Snyder, 1986]

We are all concerned, on a daily basis, about what other people think of us, although we tend to feel that not everybody's opinion is of equal importance. When it really does matter what others think, we try to create and maintain a good impression: this is the basis of Impression Management, or the ways in which we attempt to present ourselves so that others will see us in a particular light. We might, for instance, want to appear to our colleagues at work as hard-working but fun; to our boss as conscientious and professional; to our parents as independent and self-sufficient; and to our friends as caring and lively. We create these images by subconsciously or consciously engaging in Impression Management techniques; as if we were actors on a stage, constantly performing to create suitable images for our changing audiences. [Source: Goffman, 1959]

It is not enough, however, to do this sporadically, and for the benefit of certain people alone: this chapter will show you not only how to manage the image you project but also the importance of doing this continually. For the true Impression Manager, everybody's opinion counts, all the time.

Personal PR

Personal PR is more proactive than Impression Management. Examples of Impression Management behaviour include smiling or dressing appropriately every day at work, whereas Personal PR might be reserved for when we seek promotion, or for when we are attempting to rescue a bad image.

Impression Management

Although some Impression Management activities occur subconsciously, to really get on in the workplace it is vital to recognise that true Impression Management is a skill that needs to be learned. The first step in learning how to manage your image is to accept the fact that, from now on, you will have to continually monitor your feelings, thoughts and preferences in such a way that they will have the primary benefit of enhancing your image.

While everybody cares about their projected image to some extent, most of us don't often consciously think carefully enough about the impression we are creating. Only when it really matters what the other person thinks of us (for example, in a new romantic relationship), do we engage in strong impression-managing behaviour. However, for the modern worker it always matters what people (and particularly an employer) think.

Isn't That Deceitful?

Some people feel that such an approach is deceitful and Machiavellian, but this is a misunderstanding of the core concept. Impression Management is about enhancing the skills and abilities you already have, not pretending that you have them; it's about extolling your virtues as opposed to making them up. In no way should Impression Management involve creating an alter-ego; it simply means that you can display your skills and your virtues to those around you.

Impression Management also requires a deep self-understanding so that any discrepancy between the real self and the 'desired' self is acknowledged. There should not, however, be a huge character gap between the impression you are creating and the 'real you'. According to a psychological theory called 'person-environment fit', in an ideal job your personality, skills and abilities should fit the environment like a glove. If you are having to create a false persona, you will find it exhausting; it could be that you are in the wrong job, or simply do not 'fit' that particular 'environment'. [Source: Walker-Burt, 1980]

Managing your impression successfully also relies upon empathy with those around you so that you can become conscious of their reactions. You are then aware of the appropriate way to behave and able to successfully manage the image you are projecting. Such behaviour not only directly advances your career, it also reflects a respect for the person or people with whom you are interacting. If you care about managing your impression, it shows that you care deeply about their opinion. You can be bothered to make the effort. They are worth impressing.

The six-part plan that follows provides the basic Impression Management techniques that you will need to create and maintain the right image at work in order to get ahead and stay ahead.

2. First Impressions Count

Creating and maintaining the desired impression is achieved through much more subtle ways than those which operate on a conscious level: your non-verbal behaviour is also crucial.

Because we are bombarded with images, information, words, stories and facts throughout our daily lives, we cope by trying to mentally organise such input into categories. We may categorise some inputs as 'useful', others as 'useless'. Some of these inputs will be stored in our memories for later use; others will be discarded almost immediately.

A similar mental categorisation act is performed on people, too. In the busy, information-loaded lives of the late twentieth century, the mental short cuts made by taking snap categorisation decisions save precious time: thus it can be instantly concluded that this person is hard-working, or that one is lazy. Because they need to be processed quickly, these decisions are often based on the most salient evidence, however flimsy. The 'primacy effect', as it is often called, is not easily overcome by information to the contrary gleaned later. [Source: Cooper and Robertson, 1998] Interviewers, for example, often make up their minds about a candidate within the first few minutes of an interview. [Source: Spingbett, 1958]

Rightly or wrongly, your carefully prepared responses, brilliant report, or intelligent comments, despite their importance, will make less of a lasting impression than what you wear, your grooming, or your body language.

What You Wear

Most offices have one of five categories of dress code, and you will be expected to conform to one of the following.

Type of Dress Code	Deciphering the Code
The Power-Dress Code.	Everyone dresses to impress and to look bigger, taller and more important than the next person.
The Suit Code.	Everyone is expected to wear smart suits all the time.
The Non-Suit-But-Still-Smart Code.	Suits are not worn, but jackets, ties and trousers or skirts and jackets are worn.
The Suited-Manager-Non-Suited-Junior Code.	The managers wear suits but the less senior people are not expected to dress quite so smartly.
The Anything-Goes Code.	Dress code varies according to individual preference and circumstance.

If you look like a student, you will be treated as such; similarly, you will be treated like a responsible, efficient manager if you dress like a responsible, efficient manager. If yours is an 'Anything Goes' Code, always dress smartly, rather than in your torn jeans; you should always dress as you would like to be seen if the CEO, Managing Director or an important client were to pop in for a chat.

Golden Rule
Dress for the job you want, not the job you have; and always dress at the smartest end of your dress code.

Grooming

There is little point wearing your smartest jacket if it is topped with a head of lank, badly cut hair. The basics of grooming are about personal hygiene, cleanliness and 'dress hygiene'. The following may seem obvious points, but you should never underestimate the importance of:

* washing your hair regularly.

* keeping your hair neat and professional-looking. It is distracting to have to toss your hair over your shoulder, or have it fall into your line of vision every time you turn to the computer.

- bathing or showering daily.

- wearing newly washed clothes.

- ironing those clothes that require ironing.

- wearing delicate rather than overpowering deodorants, perfume or aftershave. Your scent should not overpower at 20 yards.

Body Language

Research shows that more than half of the information communicated in a message comes from body language [Source: Mehrabian, 1970]:

Example:

Worker 1 says, 'I'll get it to you by Thursday'. Her arms are held out, palms upwards, and she shrugs her shoulders.

Worker 2 says, 'I'll get it to you by Thursday'. His arms are crossed, and his body is turned away.

The words are the same, but the body language of both workers is saying something completely different. Worker 1 is saying, 'I'll do my best, but it will be hard', while Worker 2 communicates resentment.

The line between positive and negative body language is sometimes hard to distinguish; you should remain conscious of it in all the following work situations.

In Introductions

Positive Body Gesture	Impression Received
Offering a firm handshake and a smile.	Conveys self-confidence and interest.
Shaking the hand 3–5 times.	Any less or more indicates nervousness.
Direct eye contact.	Conveys interest and self-confidence.
Offering a hug or kiss to the opposite gender.	Suggests feelings of warmth and friendliness. This should only be used with people with whom a warm relationship has *already* been developed.
Negative Body Gesture	Impression Received
Failure to offer hand.	Could suggest coldness and disinterest. Take the initiative.
Glancing away.	Suggests more interest in what is going on elsewhere.
Turning your hand so that your palm faces down in the handshake, forcing their hand down.	Creates an impression of dominance and a wish to take control.
Offering 'over-familiar' handshakes that involve two hands; grasping the wrist, elbow or shoulder; or putting an arm around the shoulder.	Conveys extra feeling, but unless the feeling is mutual, these actions can be seen negatively, as over-friendliness or intrusive behaviour.

In Meetings

Positive Body Gesture	Impression Received
Pen poised in hand.	Creates a positive impression: you are eager and alert.
Chin resting on thumb (not hand).	Conveys interest and enthusiasm.
Making occasional notes.	Shows that you find the conversation relevant and useful.
Moving forward in chair.	Do this to show that you are especially interested in a particular point.
Putting the head to one side.	Shows interest in what is being said.
Hand-clenching: above the table or leaning on the elbows.	Creates the impression that you are interested in the proceedings.
Negative Body Gesture	**Impression Received**
Hand-clenching: hands dropped on lap.	Conveys an impression of boredom or anxiety.
Frequent touching of hair, mouth, eyes and neck.	Implies discomfort with what is happening or what is being said.
Face in hands.	Creates a clear impression of boredom.
Gazing out of the window.	Clearly says 'I am not interested'.
Tapping a pen or fingers on the desk.	Suggests that you are bored, irritated or impatient to leave.
Folded arms.	A comfortable position, but one that inevitably creates an impression of boredom or even hostility. You should always avoid folded arms in meetings.
Head down, eyes looking up.	Suggests disapproval or timidity.
Sitting with both hands behind the head.	Creates an image of superiority, especially when the person is also leaning back in the chair. Avoid this stance.
Picking at clothes.	Implies disapproval or boredom.

In Presentations

Positive Body Gesture	Impression Received
Eye contact with members of the audience.	Shows confidence.
Leaning on the podium with both hands.	Shows confidence.
Occasional walking around.	Shows a certainty about the material being presented.
One hand in trouser/jacket pocket.	Suggests that you are relaxed.
Stiff, formal posture.	Suggests lack of confidence.
Negative Body Gesture	**Impression Received**
Standing behind the podium with arms tightly folded across the chest.	Implies defensiveness or acute lack of confidence.
Pacing quickly.	Conveys nervousness.
Talking to the wall, overhead projector or flipchart.	Implies that you lack experience. Always face the audience.
Overuse of hands.	Shows nervousness.

In the Office

Body Gesture	Impression Received
'Open' body language, such as uncrossed arms or legs.	Shows that you have nothing to hide or fear.
Relaxed stance (for example, one hand in the pocket, leaning on the desk, sitting back on a chair).	Gives the impression that you are comfortable with your work and are happy to be questioned on it.
'Responsive' body language (that which responds to the other person – if they are sitting, you might too, and so on).	Shows that your ideas and thoughts are in tune with those of the other individual.
Standing too close to another person.	Invades personal space: the other will receive a negative impression of you, without really knowing why.
Pointing.	Creates an aggressive impression. Many theme park workers in America are advised to direct people with an open palm rather than pointing. [Source: Van Maanen and Kunda, 1989].
Hands on hips or waist.	Creates an impression of annoyance, aggression or anger.

A Short Note on Personal Style
You must be aware that, in some industries, visible stylistic eccentricities may create an impression of a less-than-efficient worker; if you espouse a more unconventional look, you may not be happy working in a bank. On the other hand, you might be ideally suited for a job in the media, arts or record industries. Similarly, avoid wearing badges, buttons or pins, especially those with political or controversial messages, unless your company openly supports the views in question. Finally, reserve baseball caps for playing sport: they simply aren't appropriate for the office.

3. The Importance of Being Professional

Being professional is... the difference between doing a job well enough to warrant your salary and doing a job as if you were on work experience.

Being professional is... doing the job to the best of your ability, on time, within the resource parameters allocated, without adversely affecting colleagues, without letting anyone down, and in an efficient and ordered manner.

Being professional is... being able to give an accurate appraisal of work in progress: when it should be completed; what has been done; and what still needs doing.

The emphasis here is, once again, on appearance. Appearing to be professional takes being professional one step further. There are many professional workers who produce good quality work, yet do not appear to be professional because their methods are disorganised or haphazard. Projecting an image of professionalism will enhance your career and make a lasting impression on colleagues and superiors.

Introductions
The first step towards being seen as a competent and professional worker lies in the manner in which you behave during an introduction.

- Remember the handshake rules.

- Repeat the person's name in your conversation. For example, you might say, "Hello, John"; or, "Nice to meet you, John".

- If the name was unusual, or you didn't catch it, ask them to repeat it. If you are still unsure, you could ask them to spell it.

- Don't just stand there after the introduction. Ask a question about their job role; tell them what you do, or will be doing, in the company. The secret to small talk is to ask questions or give full answers to any questions you may be posed.

- After an introduction, you may refer to your peer group – and probably your immediate boss – by their first names. With regard to more powerful figures of authority – chairpersons and similar – formality of address is recommended. Ask a reliable colleague what the best form of address is. Never assume that the office banter will supply you with the correct method of addressing the Managing Director. Sir Giles is unlikely to appreciate being called 'Giles-baby'.

In the Office

Your attitude to introductions has given an appearance of professionalism that will no doubt stick with all those who have met you. Now you must sustain the image of being professional during day-to-day office life.

File papers in clearly labelled in-trays. Your boss, seeing the piles in your out-tray and in your in-tray, will realise that you have achieved a great deal but still have plenty to keep you going.

- Avoid 'wearing your heart on your sleeve'. You may be worried, upset or angry about something, but these emotions should not be displayed like a badge. Make the effort to hide them, and people will think you are competent, mature and focused on your work.

- Always be punctual. Being late creates an impression of disorganisation and laziness. If you are delayed, ring in to explain the problem.

- Meet deadlines. Do the work when you say you will do it, or, if this becomes impossible, explain the reasons for this well in advance.

- Keep your workspace neat and clutter-free. This won't necessarily produce better work, but it does create an impression of efficiency and organisation.

- Ensure that all work is well-presented and free of spelling mistakes. Again, this reflects an ability to do the job well. Presentation is everything, and the poor presentation of a piece of work will overshadow its good points; a bad impression is not easily overcome.

- Follow up meetings or phone calls with a letter clarifying what was agreed.

There are no real downsides to appearing professional. There are, however, certain things of which you should always be aware.

- If you are under too much pressure, you need to do something about it. Meeting every deadline with a smile on your face will not allow your boss to appreciate the pressure you are under.

- Desks that are too neat and tidy and a steady meeting of deadlines can create the impression that you have less to do than your more cluttered and occasionally-late-with-deadlines colleagues. You should find a balance between appearing professional and appearing under-worked.

Working at Working Hard
Although Impression Management is frequently concerned with appearance, if your semblance of hard work is really concealing laziness, Impression Management will not be able to disguise this. Ideally you must work hard and be seen to be working hard.

- Present your boss with the fruits of your labour at regular intervals.

- To convey the impression that you are in a hurry and anxious to get on with your work, do not linger in the corridors.

- Carry papers or folders with you, even if you are just going to the coffee machine. This conveys the impression that you are always working.

- Develop networking systems with people outside the company who are in the same line of work as you, in order to provide learning opportunities.

The 'halo and horns effect' refers to the manner in which a good salient point (such as presentation) will imply to most individuals that the less salient aspects (such as content) are also good – 'halo effect'. If the presentation is poor, the 'horns effect' means that we assume the content will be similarly poor. [Source: Cooper and Robertson, 1998]

4. The Importance of Being Enthusiastic

"I am looking for the worker whose every action is the equivalent to them banging their fist on my desk and saying, 'I want this job! I love this job!' In other words, what I want to see more than anything else is enthusiasm."

Michael, Personnel Officer

In the ideal world – or job – you would be continually full of enthusiasm, practically swinging from the light fittings, bursting with boundless energy. The reality is different – emotion, stress, tiredness and task dissatisfaction can all impede enthusiastic behaviour. Similarly, you may be highly enthusiastic, but are simply not conveying this to your colleagues and superiors who remain oblivious. The worker who recognises the importance of Impression Management, however, will have a variety of ways in which to demonstrate enthusiasm at all times and in all situations.

Stress – emotional or work-related – is a common feature of working life today. Later sections of this book deal with stress and coping mechanisms, and how to manage your emotions at work.

- Volunteer for, and accept, tasks – particularly the unpopular ones.

- Ask for feedback or advice; and thank those who offer it to you.

- Ask relevant and considered questions.

- Arrive early at your desk; work late if required (when reasonable).

- Volunteer to attend appropriate courses.

- Keep your body language 'open' – don't fold your arms or slouch.

- Be cheerful, with an upbeat 'hello' in the morning and a 'have a nice evening' at the end of the day.

- Smile!

> Beware of being over-enthusiastic! One manager who employed a new worker was bemused and somewhat intimidated by their unfailing enthusiasm. He said, 'It was like a whirlwind had burst into the building and got trapped there.'

Avoid behaviour which, though enthusiastic, will not impress or advance your career or will irritate your colleagues.

- Don't volunteer for tasks inappropriately. If your boss mentions how dusty the windows are, don't rush forward with a feather duster. This will only belittle your capabilities. Similarly, don't offer to take a top-level meeting on your first day. Make sure that the tasks you volunteer for are within your capabilities and job remit: although this does not mean that making the tea should be beneath you. But be wary of getting stuck buying the sandwiches or taking the minutes every time. [Insert designed reference to Chapter 8.]

- Do have confidence in your opinions and abilities: constantly asking for feedback will make you appear unsure and nervous.

- Don't work late if it isn't necessary: you may create the impression that you are a slow and inefficient worker.

- Modify your behaviour to the situation in which you find yourself. Smiling is important, but grinning widely while hearing bad news about sales figures will not endear you to anyone.

Positivity

While you wish to be positive you don't want to be a 'yes' person. Appearing positive should not involve suppressing your views, intelligence or creativity, but should allow you to present criticisms in a constructive manner.

Research shows that what managers look for most in an employee is enthusiasm. [Source: Rafaeli and Sutton, 1989; Hochschild, 1983; Forbes and Jackson, 1980]

Example:
A new marketing programme is suggested, but it is badly flawed.
Non-Impression Manager's response: Sneers at the plan and declares it unworkable.
Impression Manager's response: Enthuse about the overall plan first, then gently introduce suggestions for improvement.

Example:
The boss asks for an opinion on a colleague.
Non-Impression Manager's response: Comments that the individual in question has a hot temper.
Impression Manager's response: Accentuates the positive first, then suggests aspects about them that may be 'misunderstood', wrongly interpreted, or which detract from their better characteristics.

Ideas from others should be visibly accepted using nods and smiles, while any comments you make should demonstrate that you are looking for the good in an idea or situation, at least initially, before weighing in with some carefully chosen words of criticism.

Example:
"That's a good idea – it must have taken some planning. The only reservation I have is that our target market may not be sophisticated enough at this stage."

Golden Rule
Never, *never* make disparaging or negative remarks about other workers or ideas in front of a group of co-workers as a topic of conversation.

5. The Art of Ingratiation

What is Ingratiation?
As an Impression Management technique, the aim of ingratiation is to do more than just create a good impression – used effectively, ingratiation will encourage the recipient not only to like you, but to behave in a way that will benefit your career. The three techniques to master are Opinion Agreement, Doing Favours, and Flattery.

Opinion Agreement
The more two people resemble each other in opinion, the more they will like one another. Similarly, the more someone confirms that your views are correct, the more you tend to like that person. Agreeing with the opinions of others is a double whammy: it increases the chances that they will like you; and it confirms to them that their opinions must be right, which further increases their regard for you.

Example:
The individual states that they are a vegetarian.
Impression Manager's Response: You claim to eat little red meat.

Example:
The individual states that they are an Arsenal supporter.
Impression Manager's Response: You agree that they have some of the finest players around.

On the other hand, you should not simply agree with everything the other person says – no one wants an obvious 'yes' person. It is better to occasionally disagree, especially on the matters that are less important to the other person. It can be effective, also, to allow yourself to be persuaded to their point of view – everyone likes to believe they can convince others that they are right!

Doing Favours

Doing a favour for others relies heavily on the psychological reciprocity rule, which states that if someone does something nice for us, we feel indebted to return their goodwill. Doing someone a favour is another double whammy – it creates the impression that we are generous, while paving the way for these acts of kindness to be reciprocated.

Flattery

This is a simple form of ingratiation, but one that should be pursued with discretion: the wise Impression Manager will not appear to offer flattery or compliments too easily. Any flattery, when offered, should be specific and original; otherwise, it will sound false and insincere.

Golden Rule
Find something you can truthfully admire so that you can do it with sincerity.

6. The Art of Self-Handicapping

If things go wrong at work – we fail to meet a deadline, we produce a poor piece of work, we fail to make a sale – it is normal human behaviour to try to have an excuse to hand. The deadline wasn't met because you had so much on/were ill only last week/had to care for your sick mother. The work was poor quality because you were under so much stress/the computer broke down/you were so busy helping your colleagues.

The clever Impression Manager goes one step further by creating the conditions necessary to have a ready-made excuse. Thus they actually do handicap their performance in the manner dictated by their excuse. [Source: Rosenfeld, 1995]

Example:

You have an important presentation to make in front of some important people, including your boss. You are worried that it will not go down well, and you decide (perhaps even subconsciously) to self-handicap. In other words, you create an excuse ready to use if things go badly. You might create a hectic schedule of meetings and travel during the days leading up to the presentation. Should things then go wrong, you can then simply say, "My schedule left me no time to prepare."

Cautionary Note

The problem with self-handicapping is, of course, that you are increasing the chances of failure. Thus self-handicapping as an Impression Management skill should be used rarely, and is best relied upon when the situation is unavoidable.

7. Never Too Late: Rescuing A Bad Impression

"I had been in my new job for a couple of months when I was taking some mail to the mail-room. The pile of mail to go out was huge and teetering with big brown envelopes. I was concerned that my little letter would fall off or be lost, so I slipped it into the middle of the pile, ready to be franked. I turned round to see my boss watching me – it was clear he thought I had been sending a personal letter through the office mail and that was why I had hidden it. I was mortified."

Alison, Account Executive

"I once stayed off work by calling in sick. I had a rotten cold, but started to feel better later in the day. I decided to go to town and get some cold medicine from the chemist. While I was in town, I had a look in some shops and saw a great dress, which I bought. Of course I then bumped into my boss's secretary who was on an errand. She was the one I had spoken to earlier to say I was sick... yet there I was, laden down with shopping bags. I'm sure she would have told my boss that I was skiving."

Suzanne, Assistant Brand Manager

"I was going through a really difficult domestic period at a time that I had just been promoted. My wife had walked out and threatened divorce. My young kids were devastated. I spent a lot of time on the phone in those weeks trying to sort out my mess. Things improved and we are back together, but I have somehow never been able to shake off my reputation as being someone who is always taking personal calls at work."

Philip, Sales Manager

Even skilled Impression Managers can do or say something that can send their carefully cultivated image haywire. If this has happened to you, don't panic. Bad impressions can be rescued and turned around.

Example:

British Airways went from having an extremely poor image to having one of the best, associated with quality, professionalism and service.

Example:

Coca-Cola damaged their image by changing the formula of their drink, but managed to rescue it by reintroducing the traditional formula. [Source: Hartley, 1992]

This two-step plan will help to rescue a bad impression, and is based upon strategies used by companies in response to a public relations crisis.

Step 1: Apologise and explain
If you are able to respond quickly to what has happened, do so. Meet the problem square on: don't try to pretend it never happened. Apologise if necessary (if only for the way your actions appeared) and ask to start again with a clean slate.

There is a fine – but important – line between apologising and making an excuse. Making an excuse tends to be seen in a negative light as untruthful or false; an apology, however, is honest and sincere. Combining apologising and an excuse in the right way will explain your behaviour, apologise for it, and go a long way towards reinstating that good impression.

- Make sure what you are saying is truthful, or at least largely truthful. Don't attempt to rescue a bad impression with a tissue of lies.

- Make sure that your apology-excuse is not something that you have used repeatedly. If you have a reputation for always being late, don't start your apology with the same old oversleeping/missed the train excuses. Instead, start by saying that you have mistakenly not regarded time-keeping as a priority which is why you were always late.

- Be suitably solemn and serious. For an apology to be accepted it must be perceived as sincere.

Step 2: Create a strategy
"I once made the mistake of telling an inappropriate joke at work. It was a racist joke and I was reported to the boss who did not take kindly to such things. He was worried that I was supervising 20 people, including some black and Asian people, and that I would be discriminatory. As it happens, I do not consider myself racist and always judge people on their ability alone. However, I could see how my remark would have created the impression that I was racist, so I set about rescuing the impression I had created. First of all, I apologised to my boss and showed him that I realised I had been wrong to make the joke. I tried to reassure him of my policy towards equal opportunities and told him that I intended to send round a memo to those who had heard my joke, informing them that I felt that I was wrong to make it. I made a commitment never to make a racist joke again, whether at or away from work, and not even to tolerate listening to other people's racist jokes. I think my boss was impressed by my sincerity and the fact that I didn't just make an excuse or play down my blunder."

Josh, Marketing Manager

This person took positive action, sending memos, and talking directly to his boss. Additional strategies include:

- setting up meetings; telling people that you feel you have created a bad impression, and asking them to allow you to redress it.

- explaining why such an impression was created – but never blame others.

- always declaring what you are going to do to ensure that the bad impression will no longer be justified in the future.

Chapter Checkpoint

You should now understand:

- that Impression Management and Personal PR are about creating an appropriate impression at all times.
- the role of personal appearance in impression maintenance: how to use your clothes, appearance and body language to create the right impression.
- what it means to be professional and how to appear professional at all times.
- the importance of visible enthusiasm and positivity and how to convey them.
- the risks and benefits of ingratiation and self-handicapping.
- how to rescue a bad impression.

In the Next Chapter

How to understand the unwritten rules and hidden codes associated with your working environment.

Further Reading

Molloy, J. T., *Women Dress for Success* (London: Foulsham, 1980).

Pease, A., *Body Language: How to Read Others' Thoughts by Their Gestures* (London: Sheldon Press, 1984).

Hughes, V., *Self-Presentation Skills* (Basingstoke: Macmillan, 1991).

Robson, P., *Body Language* (London: Watts, 1995).

Chapter Two

The Rules: Understanding and Fitting into your Work Environment

The Aim

Career advancement – getting in, getting on.

Few of us work in total isolation from others or are oblivious to the work environment. In the new millennium, workers must not only acknowledge the nature of the surrounding environment, they must also incorporate it into their career strategy. This means taking the time to learn, understand and assimilate the rules, etiquette and protocol that make up the work environment.

All environments have their rules or norms, as does any group of human beings. The trick for fitting into such an environment or group is not only to learn what the rules are but also to attempt to 'obey' them as smoothly as possible.

Firstly, then, you should know about the two different varieties of rules: written and unwritten. Once you are able to distinguish between the two, the complexities of each will be easier to understand. The written rules, however, are quite simple to work out; it is the unwritten rules that are more complicated.

Most of the unwritten rules are located within the office culture. Being able to read and understand office culture will enable you to fit into the environment and also to profit from what you know to be the unofficial – yet crucial – code that is your office's culture.

As well as understanding the general culture (values, norms, and so on) in which you are working, you also need to be able to read the emotional culture of your organisation: 'Warm', 'Cool', or 'Have A Nice Day?'

Another set of unofficial rules can be found within office conduct. Certain types of behaviour are simply not acceptable at work, and thus it is important to know exactly what office etiquette is, and of what it consists.

Unwritten rules do not, however, exist in just the office workspace. They also govern those events which cross the boundaries between work and social life – office parties, conferences, business lunches, and so on. Once again, knowing such rules will prove extremely useful as your career progresses.

The office workspace itself is much less clearly-defined than it was 20 years ago. With teleworkers, flexitime, freelancers, and so on, a whole new set of codes has sprung up for those whose working environment is not office-based. If you are such a person, you will find this collection of unwritten rules particularly useful.

The Written Rules

The word 'Written' is something of a misnomer, because not all these rules will actually be found on paper. 'Written' here means 'formally acknowledged'. In other words, these are the openly practised rules of the company; those which have been consciously devised by the organisation; which will be made clear to each employee; and which all must follow.

The Unwritten Rules

This set of rules will never be officially acknowledged but they can be found everywhere, from office parties to board meetings. They are more complex and less obvious elements of working life to which you must adhere if you are to move onwards and upwards within your chosen career.

1. The Written Rules

These easy-to-understand rules will usually appear in several different places:

- within your written job contract. These rules will tell you whom to inform if you are sick; when to get a doctor's note; how to take out grievance procedures; what constitutes a sackable offence; what the disciplinary procedures are; how many days' holiday you are allowed and so on. If any of the rules within your job contract aren't clear or you feel that important ones have not been mentioned, make enquiries to your supervisor.

- within policy statements. These stipulate the company policy towards answering the phone; how long it is acceptable to keep customers waiting; how to address senior workers; and so forth. Again, if part of the company policy is not clear, ask a reliable colleague or supervisor for further information.

- during job induction courses. Here any new recruits are informed about important rules, including how long to take over lunch breaks; whether it is acceptable to eat at desks; where to obtain office supplies and so on.

That was the simple part. The unwritten rules are equally – if not more – important, but far more difficult to understand and absorb.

2. The Unwritten Rules – Office Culture

Using the same techniques as those used by organisational consultants, the following section will enable you to define and profit from the culture of your particular working environment.

What Is 'Office Culture'?

The culture of an office describes what the organisation is about, what it stands for and where it is going.

An organisation's culture provides unwritten guidelines about how to behave, think and feel. Reading and identifying office culture helps reduce uncertainty and complexity within the work environment.

Identifying the office culture is complex and often fraught with peril. There are many psychologists and consultants who spend months attempting to understand an office's culture, using questionnaires, observations and interviews. So how can you, a non-expert, read your office culture? The following guide should allow you to make a very basic diagnosis of the rules which dominate your working environment.

The Elements of Office Culture

Environment

The physical layout of the offices (for example, if they are open-plan, if there are large offices for managers, and so on); the use of decoration, plants, pictures, and such.

Values

The aims and ideals to which the company or organisation appears to aspire: for example, product quality, low absenteeism or high efficiency. These values are often communicated in 'vision statements', annual reports or literature of a similar nature.

Philosophy

The policies or beliefs of the company towards employees' treatment of each other, or how customers are treated.

Norms

These are (usually unwritten) standards of behaviour or guidelines on how to behave.

Behaviour

The observable behaviour of employees. Examples include the language used (whether it is politically correct; if individuals swear or use outspoken tones; and so on), and the rituals engaged in (such as taking lunch at certain times; going for after-work drinks; and so forth).

Bearing in mind all of the above, the following five-part assessment will enable you to diagnose your office culture sufficiently to understand the basic rules. The process, like the elements above, begins at the surface of the organisation and moves inward to the 'subconscious' of the company.

Task 1: Study the Environment

The physical environment of the company makes a statement to the outside world; to the customer; and to you, the employee. Ask yourself the following questions and if your answer is 'yes' make a note of the corresponding number:

Are the buildings new and uniform with sharp angles, or with lots of glass and neutral colours?	6
Is the building old-looking, rather than new and modern?	3
Are head offices more modern and gleaming than other offices?	1
Are there barriers or systems in place to prevent unauthorised people entering the buildings?	6
Are the buildings and offices clearly labelled with directions provided?	5
Is there a reception area, with chairs for visitors?	5
Do all levels of staff eat in the same facilities and park in the same areas?	2
Are there separate car-parking facilities for management and employees?	1
Are the offices open-plan, with managers having their own offices?	1
Do managers work with their office doors open?	2
Are personal possessions on desks discouraged?	4
Do managers have family photographs or personal objects on their desks?	3
Do people wear designer clothes or have 'executive toys' on their desks?	4
Are there statements of customer care posted on the walls?	5
Are there unusual decorations such as sculptures or wacky quotes or advertisements for unusual classes such as Japanese art or aromatherapy?	3

Task 2: Establish the Values – Read Company Literature

What the company says about itself can reveal much about the value-element of its culture.

Do employees contribute to the written text?	2
Is it written by management only?	1
Does it highlight different or unusual working practices (such as teleworking)?	3
Does it have solo pictures of senior management but group pictures of lower level staff?	1
Does it mention customers or stakeholders?	5
Does the literature request suggestions (on any aspect of work life) or input from all staff?	3
Is it restricted to information regarding work-performance?	4
Does it include any reminders of the rules?	6
Does it appear to remonstrate for breaches of rules?	6
Does it demonstrate responsiveness to employees' views?	2
Does it list awards or the other achievements of employees?	4
Are any pieces of literature sent out to customers, clients or stakeholders?	5
Does it make any reference to customer service standards or ways in which to improve customer service?	5.

Task 3: Establish the Philosophy – How Are Customers and Visitors Greeted?

Look around you and note the manner in which the company presents itself to those outside the organisation; what image does it wish to project?

Is the reception area formal?	6
Is it informal and relaxed?	2
Is it elegant?	5
Is it tatty?	3
Is there an extensive signing-in procedure for visitors?	6
Are the receptionists uniformed or in smart suits?	4
Do receptionists/secretaries or administrators greet visitors for managers?	1
Do only lower-level staff greet their own visitors?	1
Do all staff greet their own visitors?	2
Do receptionists have many other tasks besides greeting visitors?	4
Are visitors kept waiting to see senior managers?	1
Is the waiting time to see any member of staff kept to a minimum?	2
Are visitors steered away from meeting anyone other than the appointed staff member?	4
Do staff members perch on tables or chair arms when talking to clients or within sight of clients?	3

Task 4: Establish the Norms – Chat to Colleagues

Ask a range of employees about the history of the company: what its values are; what its good and bad points are; and what is needed to succeed in that working environment. Questions should include the following:

Do employees refer to management on first-name terms?	2
Do you detect an 'us and them' attitude?	1
Do they take risks?	3
Do they appear to be unconventional?	3
Do they 'tell tales' or speak negatively about each other?	4
Do they complain of excessive red tape?	6
Are there senior levels of management to whom no one ever speaks?	1
Do employees feel free to make criticisms to managers?	2
Do they speak in terms of doing better, selling more, performing the best?	4
Do they feel that the customer is treated well by the company?	5
Do they treat customers with respect?	5
Do they complain of excessive red tape?	6

Task 5: Observe and Establish Behaviour

Observe how people behave, how they spend their time, with whom they interact, and so on; it can speak volumes about the office culture. Ask yourself:

Are people cliquey?	4
Is there a lot of gossip?	4
Do people swear a lot?	4
Do they do favours for each other?	2
Do people work out of loyalty/belief in the company's values?	3
Do they treat senior staff with more respect than subordinates?	1
Do they treat everyone with respect?	2
Do people talk negatively about bosses behind their backs?	1
Do they make appointments with managers in advance?	1
Do they treat customers well?	5
Does customer-contact work take up most of their time?	5
Do they always seem to be following rules or protocol?	6
Do they challenge and question things frequently?	2
Do they spend little time on paperwork?	3
Do they spend a lot of time completing forms or paperwork?	6

The most frequently-selected numbers will define the category to which your organisation belongs. If no one category stands out, there is probably no strong defining culture – you should thus amalgamate the most frequently-ticked categories.

In addition, some organisations will have more than one culture: perhaps different departments have different unwritten rules; or the culture may vary from location to location within, say, a national firm. The categories most regularly selected may well apply to your department or branch only, and are not necessarily representative of the organisation as a whole.

Note
This is a brief and straightforward guide not designed to be comprehensive.

Mostly 1: Hierarchical Culture
You work in an environment that is very regimented, with strict hierarchical systems. Everyone is expected to know their place and respect is due to senior management.

(Unwritten) rules to remember in Hierarchical Culture
* Address senior members of staff with care and respect.

* Establish the path of communication (whether, for example, you are allowed to communicate directly with someone two levels above you, or whether you should always go through your supervisor).

- Dress code: probably 'Suit-Code' or 'Suited-Manager-Non-Suited-Junior'.
  SEE CHAPTER 1

Golden Rule
Make sure that you are seen to conform, and be very wary about challenging the status quo.

Mostly 2: Egalitarian Culture
You work in a more egalitarian environment, with a strong entrepreneurial spirit and relatively little bureaucracy.

(Unwritten) rules to remember in Egalitarian Culture
- Avoid being seen as a 'yes-person' – in this organisation it is better to challenge and question.

- Dress code: probably 'Non-Suit-But-Still-Smart'.

Golden Rule
Remember basic manners and protocol – you can probably approach anyone, but you should not go too far over your supervisor's head.

Mostly 3: Creative Culture
Your work culture is a high risk-taking and unconventional one. There is little outward sign of hierarchy, and the culture fosters the belief that too much bureaucracy squashes creativity.

(Unwritten) rules to remember in Creative Culture
- Appear slightly unconventional, and give the impression that you are always challenging and questioning.

- Avoid being argumentative simply for the sake of it.

- Avoid treating different ranks in different ways; never appear subservient.

- Dress code: probably 'Anything-Goes'.

Golden Rule
The spirit of Creative Culture is co-operative rather than competitive.

Mostly 4: Competitive Culture
This environment is highly competitive, and there is little trust between colleagues. Competition is fostered by management who encourage such a culture by offering rewards or awards.

(Unwritten) rules to remember in Competitive Culture

- Play the competitive game.

- Never reveal too much of your inner self.

- Dress Code: probably the 'Power-Dress-Code'.

Golden Rule

Even in a Competitive Culture, you should never indulge in any form of back-stabbing.

Mostly 5: Customer-Oriented Culture

Here the culture fosters goodwill towards the customer, and all behaviour should be geared accordingly.

(Unwritten) rules to remember in Customer-Orientated Culture

- The customer should always be put first.

- Anything that you have contributed towards customer loyalty will probably be rewarded.

- Always make sure that you are seen to be doing all you can towards these aims.

Golden Rule

In the Customer-Orientated Culture, the customer is always right.

Mostly 6: Bureaucratic Culture

This is a culture dominated by written rules and regulations. If you forget your work pass, you will not gain entry to the building, even if the receptionist knows you: rules will always be followed strictly.

(Unwritten) Rules to Remember in Bureaucratic Culture

- There will be large amounts of paperwork to complete.

- Corners should not be cut.

Golden Rule

In a Bureaucratic Culture, all rules must be obeyed.

A Note on Office Culture [1]: Office Layouts

Generally, the greater the status of the person, the bigger and more private their office space will be.

More important people may also be located higher up the building (elevated from the riff-raff) and will probably have corner offices with lots of windows and good views.

Within the office, those with a very high status may want to further communicate their importance by being seated on a raised platform or by having a huge desk to separate them from visitors. If you come across such an office, you should be aware that the trappings of status do matter to such people; they will want you to acknowledge their importance.

People with less status have smaller offices or are situated in an open-plan office, where their territory is less private and others can walk into their space and interrupt. The furnishing will be standardised, and each will have the same equipment or furnishings as everybody else.

Furnishings and artefacts send clear messages of their own:

- **chairs with arms say...** that you are more important thus worthy of a little more expense.

- **spare chairs say...** that you are sufficiently important to have people coming to see you – the more spare chairs the better.

- **spare chairs around a separate table say...** that you are powerful; as do the presence of extra coffee tables and bar facilities.

- **spare books and bookcases say...** that you are intelligent and well-read.

- **lots of papers, in-trays and work-stations say...** that you are very busy.

- **personal artefacts – family photos or collectors items – say...** that you have a life outside work.

A Note on Office Culture [2]: Seating Arrangements

When you visit another office, or meet with your boss, client or colleague, the seating arrangements will convey powerful messages.

Seating arrangement	What it says
Their desk separates you from the other individual.	This person is saying that they are superior to you.
One person sits at the head of a table.	This person is saying 'I am the leader'.
Two people sit at right-angles to each other.	This says 'we are equal'.
No chair is provided.	This says 'hurry up and leave'.

Golden Rule
Consider the kind of impression you want to create when you decide how you want your office to be furnished.

A Note on Office Culture [3]: Use of Time

"I worked in a mental health unit and because we were psychologists who emphasised respect for all, we decided to implement a policy which stated that we would not keep patients waiting for their appointment more than five minutes. You have to realise that this was quite radical in a National Health Service where being kept waiting 45 minutes for an appointment with a doctor or consultant was the norm. We thought the patients would be very pleased with our policy, but unfortunately it backfired on us. They started to perceive us as having lower status than the doctors. They wouldn't be late for a doctor's appointment, but they started turning up late for our appointments. And sometimes they would just not turn up, fig-uring that it didn't matter – we weren't so important. We decided to keep patients waiting deliberately, for 15 minutes on average, and this solved the problems. Patients started arriving on time again, and started valuing us more."

Belinda, Cognitive Behaviour Therapist

'Time talks', said the anthropologist Edward Hall in his book *The Silent Language*. [Source: Hall, 1959] Keeping people waiting sends out a clear message: 'I am more important than you'.

Whether or not your office culture is openly hierarchical or egalitarian, you should expect those with an obviously senior status to keep you waiting. While you would not be late for a meeting with the Managing Director, you can reasonably expect them to have been delayed or to be excessively busy and thus unpunctual.

3. The Unwritten Rules – Emotional Culture

"I have to hide my real feelings at work – I'd soon get fired if I didn't. I spend my day listening to people's problems and, quite frankly, most of them bore me silly! I am Personal Assistant to three managers and I get their problems, plus all the problems of the subordinates who keep trying to see the managers. I arrange my face in a sympathetic pose and pretend to be interested, when really I can't wait for them to leave so I can get on with my work in peace."

Sarah, PA

"I find that my emotions may stay pretty stable most of the day, but the emotions I am expected to have change from situation to situation. I am expected to be enthusiastic and interested in meetings, sympathetic but firm to customers, and dis-mayed and upset by my colleagues' personal misfortunes. It can be exhausting."

James, Accounts Manager

Not all of the office culture revolves around environment, behaviour or politics. More unwritten rules of the office environment lie in its emotional culture.

What is 'Emotional Culture'?

'Emotional culture' refers to those feelings that are expected to be felt, or at least displayed, within the organisation.

Almost every organisation has an emotional culture; thus we can rarely display our true feelings at work. Instead, we spend our days moving from one faked emotional display to another: smiling cheerfully at abusive customers; nodding enthusiastically in a boring meeting; and appearing cold and unemotional to the worker who is late yet again.

Research shows that in about a third of workplace conversations, we have to fake or act the emotion we are expected to display. [Source: Mann, 1997]

Identifying and Understanding Emotional Culture

As with office culture, learning the rules of the emotional culture involves firstly identifying the culture in which you are working, and then learning to obey the rules of that culture.

Step 1: Identifying the emotional culture

Type of Culture	Main Identifiable Features
The Totally Warm Culture.	Staff are expected to be warm and friendly to each other. Customers are to be smiled at, thanked politely and wished a pleasant day. Negative emotions such as anger or boredom are suppressed. Displays of enthusiasm and interest are desired at all times.
The Partially Warm Culture.	Staff are only expected to be 'nice' to customers. Employees are expected to be honest with each other and with their superiors. Staff are allowed to let off steam after dealing with abusive customers. Negative emotions are allowed among colleagues.
The Cool Culture.	Staff are not expected to display any emotions. Employees appear aloof and distant. Real feelings are hidden behind a neutral front.
The Cold Culture.	Only negative feelings are expressed. Positive happy emotions are suppressed. The aim is to make others feel intimidated or threatened.

Step 2: Understanding and profiting from the emotional culture
Having identified the emotional culture, you must now play the game accordingly. Your acting and Impression Management skills will come into play.

[SEE CHAPTER **1**]

- Recognise and accept that you will frequently need to act. Don't expect to feel the required emotion all the time.

- Try to put yourself in the shoes of the person with whom you are dealing: you will be better able to conjure up the appropriate response.

- Identify the emotion that you are expected to display and try to think of a situation in which you felt the same.

- Discover which outward signs indicate a particular emotion, and produce them.

- A conscious use of body language can successfully convey a feeling that you don't actually have; but beware – if you don't pay attention to it, your body language may betray what you are really feeling.

Cautionary Note
If you are constantly displaying emotions you don't feel and hiding the ones you do, psychologists believe that you risk suffering from stress and burnout. [Source: Mann, 1997]

4. The Unwritten Rules – Office Etiquette

"I had a colleague with whom I had always got on well. Suddenly I noticed that she had become rather cool towards me and things got cooler until relationships became very strained between us. I had no idea what I had done or why she was behaving like this. It also seemed that other people were being cool towards me to and I became paranoid in thinking they were all against me. I moved to a different department soon after. It wasn't until six months later that I found out – from someone else – that I hadn't repaid a small loan to this colleague. I had borrowed ten pounds once and I just forgot to give it back. That really tarnished my reputation – I would never borrow money from work colleagues again."

Beth, Assistant Brand Manager

"I was doing a huge piece of work – writing a training manual – and was always at the photocopier. People were forever poking their heads round the door and asking how long I would be. I was often in the middle of a really long run and would have to tell them to come back in 15 minutes. I once overheard a colleague refer to me as 'The Photocopier' because I was always hogging the machine! From then on I always did my stuff in small print-runs so that I could let other people in if they needed to use it."

Amir, Human Resources Manager

Awareness of office etiquette is crucial to personal success, and knowing its unwritten rules will provide you with an edge over your less enlightened colleagues.

Unlike office culture, etiquette remains the same in most working environments. The following rules may seem minor and trivial but as Beth and Amir realised, adhering to them is vital for success in the workplace.

Do:

- be punctual.
- pay up on time if you join an office lottery syndicate.
- offer to buy snacks or drinks for colleagues if you are all out together.
- see if anyone else wants anything if you are going out to get your own lunch.
- what you say you will do, when you say you will do it.
- take responsibility for your own actions – don't blame anyone else, or the equipment.
- order new office supplies if, for example, you are using the last ream of paper.
- report any equipment faults.
- take your turn making tea and coffee, if this is the policy of your organisation.
- offer some privacy to anyone using the phone in your presence by leaving the room or by gesturing for them to call you when they are free.

Don't:

- treat some people as less important than others.
- interrupt.
- make or take personal phone calls more than absolutely necessary.
- answer the phone if you already have someone with you (unless you have explained in advance that you are expecting an important call).
- borrow things without returning them.
- ask to borrow money.
- hog the photocopier or use it for copious non-work material.
- eat at your desk.
- take long lunch breaks.
- be too possessive over stationery and similar things.
- talk loudly with colleagues if others are trying to work.

5. The Unwritten Rules – When Work and Play Collide

An increasing number of work-related situations now occur outside the normal office or work environment, including office parties, residential courses and overseas work trips.

The biggest mistake that most people make at these kinds of events is to imagine that they are no longer at work, and that the normal rules and regulations therefore do not apply. This is simply not true. If anything, there may even be additional rules to follow.

Office Parties

"My experience is a common one – I went to the office party and had too much to drink. But I didn't make a pass at anyone or strip off or do any of the other things that you often hear about. In a way what I did was potentially more damaging to my career. I work in occupational health and I have access to confidential medical records. I never normally dream of revealing any information, but drink does loosen my tongue. We were gossiping at the party about a male colleague and his alleged sexual prowess. It was then that I loudly revealed that he wasn't the stud he made out to be since he had recently had a vasectomy. The guy was mortified – he was obviously very embarrassed about it and had told people he was away on holiday when he had the operation. I received a verbal warning after this incident – I don't drink at office parties now."

Naomi, Occupational Therapist

- Different rules about punctuality may apply. For example, it may be acceptable and even desirable to be half an hour late. Check the rules by asking others what time they plan to arrive.

- Dress may be a little more casual than in the office, but avoid anything too revealing, skin-tight or unusual.

- Your social skills are on show more than in the office, so remember to be courteous and polite.

- Avoid drinking too much. This is the most common pitfall of the office party, especially if the alcohol is free. Drunken passes at the boss, vomiting over the photocopier or collapsing on the nearest filing cabinet are behaviours that are unlikely to impress and will haunt you for years to come.

- Never make sexual passes at anyone. This is not a normal party – always remember that you are at work.

- The wise worker will make efforts to meet and talk to people outside their own circle. You never know when you could meet someone interesting or make a good contact.

- Use the opportunity to make contact with superiors and senior management, but don't spend the evening telling them about your achievements or trying to extract office secrets out of them.

- Always appear to be enjoying yourself, even if you can't wait to get home to a cup of cocoa.

- Offer to help with the organisation or clearing up.

Working Lunches

"I took a client out for lunch to a local restaurant that I knew was good. The meal went well and we had just started on the dessert. Suddenly, to my horror, my ex-girlfriend walked into the restaurant – I had dumped her a week previously. To my chagrin she spotted me and stormed over to give me a piece of her mind. I was very embarrassed and just did not know what to do. She told my client – who happened to be a woman – that I was a lying cheat! Luckily my client thought it was hilarious, but I could have lost the business. I have learnt my lesson – I always take clients to less local places now."

Chris, Financial Advisor

- Take many of your cues about how to behave from your host – in other words, the person who is paying. If they order an alcoholic drink, therefore, feel free to do the same; if they order a starter, you may, too… Don't choose the most expensive item on the menu if the other person is paying, but neither should you necessarily go for the cheapest. Take the lead from your companion.

- If you invited the other person, then you set the pace – and do the ordering – but there are still rules to follow. It is appropriate to offer wine with the meal, and suggest a starter and dessert.

- Generally, business is not discussed until at least after the orders have been placed, and sometimes not until after the first course. However, these rules are not rigid, especially if there is a lot to get through.

- If you are using papers or diagrams, it is usually best to bring these out after the main course, or at least between courses, rather than in the middle of eating.

- Business lunches generally last between one-and-a-half to two hours. It is a good idea to let the other person (or persons) know in advance at what time you will need to leave.

- Express some appreciation of the food, particularly if you are the guest.

Residential Courses and Conferences

All the rules mentioned already apply – as do some extra ones.

- Attend most – if not all – of the lectures. It is not a good idea to be seen to be spending more time at the bar than on the course.

- Make the most of every and any opportunity to network. Swap business cards, and stay in touch.

- As in the office, you should use your Impression Management skills to appear interested and enthusiastic during lectures, seminars or courses.

Overseas Work Trips

Once again, all the usual rules apply, but there are some extra points to note.

• Keep the receipts for everything you spend: you will need these for payment claims.

• Don't be over-, or under-extravagant in your subsistence claims. Find out before you go what your company considers to be a reasonable amount to spend per day on food.

• Similarly, find out what kind of accommodation would suit the company's budget.

• Rules about taking spouses/partners and family (at your own expense) will vary with the company, the purpose of the trip and on whether anyone from work is accompanying you. Generally, if you are going with a colleague, it is best to leave your family at home. If you do take your family (and are, perhaps, having an extended holiday afterwards), leave them out of the business meetings, unless they are specifically invited.

> **Golden Rule**
> Treat any work-related social situation as a *work* situation.

6. The Unwritten Rules – When Work and Home Collide

Not everyone will be working in an office every day. The new, flexible workplace probably consists of:

> a core office-based staff (some of whom may work flexible hours).
> a core home-based staff (teleworkers).
> a further workforce of freelancers or outsourcers to be called on when necessary. [Source: Handy, 1994]

If you are thinking about working from home or starting on flexitime it is worth thinking closely about the advantageous and disadvantageous elements of this very different working method. Once you have examined these, it is important subsequently to establish some ground rules and guidelines for working to flexible hours, or outside the office environment.

A survey of teleworkers in America found that over half worked in the evenings. [Source: Pratt, 1984]

On the Positive Side, You May

• Spend less money on travel, food, clothing, and similar work accessories.
• Be able to dress casually for work.
• Have greater control over your environment (for example, temperature).
• Be able to work from home if you are feeling unwell.

- Be uninterrupted by colleagues.
- Be able to intersperse work with recreation, thus avoiding the crowds in the supermarket or fitness club.
- Be able to work the hours that suit you.
- Have a better family life. 'Water cooler' breaks that would be spent with co-workers can be spent with family members. [Source: Nilles, 1994]
- Be able to overlap household chores with employment – for example, doing the washing while waiting for an article to print out. [Source: Hill, Hawkins and Miller, 1996]
- Be better able to handle family mini-crises – a major concern for parents. [Source: Galinsky, Bond and Friedman, 1993]

A survey in the UK in 1983 reported that 60 per cent of teleworkers named isolation as the greatest disadvantage. [Source: Huws, 1984] A great many people meet their future partners or make good friends at work. [Source: Haddon and Lewis, 1994]

On the Negative Side, You May

- Experience social isolation.
- Encounter career marginalisation. 'Visibility and office information networks are key influences on career prospects'. [Source: Haddon and Lewis, 1994] Teleworkers can become politically disadvantaged when they become 'out of flow' of such activities as resource allocation, evaluation, compensation and advancement. [Source: Turner, 1998]
- Suffer from a blurring of the division between work and home.
- Possibly feel a lack of credibility. There is a tendency that others may see you as 'not really working' if you are working at home. This may be a more significant issue for women who sometimes feel that they lose the sense of identity and independence that work provides. Like housework, the paid labour involved in teleworking may become invisible. [Source: Haddon and Lewis, 1994]
- Receive no remuneration for overtime – workers may work long hours without extra pay.
- Experience a loss of fringe benefits such as free tea and coffee, the use of a canteen, sports facilities and out of hours car-parking.
- Receive the extra costs passed on to the home-based worker such as heating, lighting, telecoms, insurance, office furniture, decorating and so on.

Some individuals maintain that the lines between work and home are so vague that the virtual office becomes a 'cyberspace sweatshop'. One teleworker interviewed said, "I am always at work... between 5 a.m. and midnight, seven days a week". [Source: Hill, Hawkins and Miller, 1996]

Dealing with the potential disadvantages of flexitime or teleworking will be easier if you use the following advice as a set of guidelines.

Rules for Freelancers
- Be meticulous about meeting deadlines. Missing one deadline can mean you being black-listed by that commissioner.

- Keep your commissioner updated on progress. This is not only polite but also reassures them that you are getting on with the job.

- Always appear bright, cheerful and willing.

- Be realistic about the work you take on – make sure you can meet deadlines.

The Rules for Office Staff with Flexi-hours
- Keep a log or record of the hours you work, if this is not done with official 'clock-ins'. One of the most common problems that managers cite with flexi-workers is the difficulty of 'controlling' or managing them and keeping checks on the hours worked.

- Plan ahead, so that other staff will know what time you will be at your desk. Flexitime does not mean working when you feel like it, but rather adopting a pattern of working to suit your circumstances. You should be able to plan your days ahead so that people will be able to contact you, and your manager will be able to keep tabs on you.

- Be reliable and punctual. Flexitime is not an excuse for shoddy work practices.

- Try to make most of your hours coincide with the times that you will be most 'visible'.

The Rules for Teleworkers
- Keep your boss or supervisor regularly informed and updated on your work. Managers frequently feel that 'they cannot manage what they cannot observe'. [Source: Wilkes, Frolick and Urwiler, 1994]

- Communicate regularly with updates (by email or post, more than by phone). This reminds your boss that you are there and increases your 'visibility'.

- Try to go into the office at least once a week, again, for reasons of visibility.

- Attend every staff meeting or team briefing. This shows that you are still a member of the team and will reduce your isolation.

- Try to keep your work and private life separate so that you are not minding the kids while working, and so on.

One manager who was used to walking the shop floor to see how his staff were doing, took to driving by teleworkers' homes to see if they were where they said they would be.

Dealing with Isolation

Companies can use a variety of approaches to compensate for isolation; for example, one UK company's teleworkers continue to be included in departmental organisation charts and on relevant circulation lists; they are invited to departmental meetings, briefings and social functions; and are listed in the company's telephone directories. Other companies recommend that teleworkers come into the office at least once each week. [Source: Di Martino and Wirth, 1990]

It is a good idea to keep a separate area for work and to dress in work clothes so that you can still maintain the psychological feeling of 'going to work'. It is also recommended that phone facilities should be organised in such a way as not to conflict with the life of the family. [Source: Di Martino and Wirth, 1990]

Chapter Checkpoint

After reading this chapter, you should:

- know the formal rules of the workplace.
- be able to read office culture.
- understand emotional culture.
- have learned basic office etiquette.
- know the rules governing work-related 'social events'.
- learned the pros, cons and rules of alternative working methods.

In the Next Chapter

Get noticed, get promoted – but always get on with the canteen staff. The importance of getting on with others in the workplace and how to stay friends with everyone.

Further Reading

Yapp, N., *Debrett's Guide to Business Etiquette: The Complete Book* (London: Hodder Headline, 1994).

Reid, A., *Teleworking: A Guide to Good Practice* (Oxford: Blackwell, 1994).

Chapter Three

From the MD to the Canteen Staff: Getting On with Everyone at Work

The Aim

Career advancement – get on with others, get on at work.

"Whenever we run interviews for new jobs here, after the interview I always ask the receptionist for her view. You'd be amazed how many people are as nice as pie to us in the interview room, but treat the receptionist like dirt, or are rude and impatient, or ask intrusive or inappropriate questions. We want people with good all-round social skills... which means they have to be able to get on with everyone."
Danielle, Communications Manager

I have a large staff base – maybe 40 people. It's funny, but they all seem to have different attitudes to different people. Some seem resentful of me as the big manager – they are always complaining and criticising. Others are all smiles to me, but can't seem to be bothered to get on with their peers – I see these people sitting on their own during breaks. Others still get on famously with their own peers, but treat cleaners and tea-ladies like servants. I also have one or two who seem to get on with everyone at all levels – they are the real movers in this company."
Chris, Production Manager

"Being able to get on with everyone is a valuable social skill. Some people are like social butterflies... they can flit smoothly from one interaction to another. They can make themselves understood to both senior managers and junior runners. Everyone likes them because they have the ability to make everyone feel valued."
Fergus, Design Manager

Few workers are able (or willing) to work hard at getting on with everyone: most limit their energies to getting on with the people who 'count'.

Big mistake. When it comes to getting on with people, everyone counts, including:

- your immediate supervisor or line-manager.

- all those in management.

- your peers and colleagues.

- people from other departments or branches within your company.

- secretaries and receptionists.

- porters, mail-workers and cleaners.

- canteen staff.

- customers, clients and stakeholders.

- suppliers or other outside companies.

- members of the media, if appropriate.

Before you can learn how to get on with everybody at work, you must first gain an essential insight into the personalities of those around you.

Once you know with whom you are working, you can begin to learn the intricacies of getting along with everybody – including the more difficult individuals.

The other person with whom you must get on is, of course, your boss: an amicable and profitable relationship with your superiors can only help your career to advance. Simultaneously, it is also essential to get along with those for whom *you* are the boss: maintaining good working relationships with subordinates will not only make your life easier, it will also show what good leadership skills you have.

Ironically, one of the greatest sources of problems with co-workers stems from friendship. How can you remain friends with someone in the workplace, while maintaining your objective and professional stance?

Finally, there are those people whose right it is to complain to you and to criticise your company – the customers. How can you keep your cool when the person in front of you is rapidly losing theirs?

Read on for your indispensable guide to making friends and making progress.

1. Getting On – With Whom Are You Working?

The astute worker will spend time analysing the people with whom they are working, and attempt to identify what makes them 'tick'. Psychologists find that this is best achieved by identifying personality, and subsequently classifying the various types of personality: not an easy task, but one that is vital for the worker who wants to get on with others, and thus get ahead.

What is Personality?

"Personality is the make-up of the person."

"Personality is not one thing – people do not have just one personality. They can be very different from one situation to another."

"It is how you behave and think."

"Personality is something you are born with. It doesn't change."

"It can change – we can alter bits of our personality as we get older."

Response by students to the question, 'What is personality?'

The term 'personality' is more than a little vague and different people will have a different understanding of the concept. The definition of personality itself has long been a subject of debate and conflict for psychologists. Suffice it to say for our purposes that although events and other people strongly influence the way in which individuals behave, people nevertheless 'always bring something of themselves to the situation'. That 'something', which represents the 'unique qualities of the individual', is personality. [Source: Hellriegel, Slocum and Woodman, 1989]

What Are the Different Types of Personality?

Some experts think that there are sixteen different 'kinds' of people, or aspects of personality; others only five. [Sources: Catell, 1987; McCrae and Costa, 1990] Certainly there is no perfect method of describing or identifying personality, although the guide that follows will go some way towards helping you to understand your colleagues.

According to one source there are more than 4000 words that can be used to describe personality. [Source: Luthans, 1992]

The four types of personality most relevant to the work situation are: Extrovert Types, Introvert Types, Type As and Type Bs.

Who Are Your Colleagues?

Personality Type	Possible Identifying Characteristics	How to behave with each type
Extrovert	Talkative; loud; likes being around people. Works better in teams than alone. Friendly.	Don't try to quash extroverts by trying to 'out-extrovert' them. Don't try to force an extrovert into roles with which they aren't comfortable, like doing tasks alone if they prefer to be with others. If they are a natural leader, don't quash this by undermining their authority or by trying to prevent them leading.
Introvert	Quiet; serious; shy. Prefers to work alone. Does not speak up or contribute much in a group.	Don't insist that introverted people contribute more. Don't force them to tell you how they feel or to be more talkative. Don't force them into team-work if they prefer to work alone.
Type A	Impatient; perfectionist; ambitious; irritable. Always in a rush. Competitive.	Don't be forever trying to slow them down. Try not to allow them to take on too much or to spend too long trying to perfect something.
Type B	Patient; easy-going; not particularly ambitious. Takes things slowly. Less keen to work all hours.	Don't try to force a Type B to be competitive. Type Bs are likely to take their time to do things.

Many companies use personality testing as a means of assessing prospective employees. Such tests are usually only available to qualified organisational psychologists for selection purposes.

2. Getting On – with Colleagues

It is a strange situation: you are flung into the middle of a diverse group of people, with whom you may have nothing in common other than the fact that you work for the same firm.

The Myth: it is possible to like everyone and for everyone to like you.

The Reality: you may have to work hard at getting on with your colleagues; and you may well find yourself facing, and working with, people who are – at the very least – difficult to get on with.

How Can I Get On with My Colleagues?

Continual practice of the following four-step plan will help to maintain a good and harmonious relationship with all your workmates.

Step 1: Do as you would be done by

It's a simple – and biblical – idea, but it works. Whenever you do or say something, consider whether you would like this to be said or done to you. If not, simply don't do or say it.

Note, however, that everybody is different, and what may not affect you could profoundly affect a colleague. If you are in any doubt about how to treat a work-mate, simply ask.

Example:

Colleague X has just given a presentation during which she demonstrated poor verbal skills (using lots of 'ums' and 'ahhs', with poor use of visual aids, and so on). Do you tell her? You may welcome such feedback, but it could destroy Colleague X's confidence.

Solution:

Ask Colleague X a carefully phrased question to discover her receptiveness to peer feedback; or lead gently into the feedback whilst gauging her reaction carefully, and subsequently making the necessary adjustments to your feedback.

Step 2: Give them the benefit of the doubt

"I lost an important piece of work because my computer crashed and I had not saved the work on to disk. This was a cardinal sin in my firm – we are always being told to save and back-up our work. I didn't want to admit to my manager that I had been so stupid, so I set about re-doing the work. I stayed until 1.30 a.m. to complete it, and the next day I told my colleague what had happened. Two days later, my manager made a snide comment to me about saving my work – it was obvious he knew, and it could only have been my colleague who told him. I went mad and told

my colleague exactly what I thought of him. His defence was that he thought our manager knew about it, and he only mentioned it because he thought we should install some zip facilities to enable us all to back-up our work on the hard drive. When I calmed down, I realised that my colleague had meant no harm, but it was too late to take back the air of mistrust that my outburst had created."

Pamela, Development Assistant

Things will always happen at work to upset you. Unlike Pamela, you must resist the temptation to explode, and instead give the individual the benefit of the doubt, assuming that they were not acting out of malicious intent.

You should, of course, approach the individual in an assertive manner; but you must avoid being accusatory. Remember – it is very difficult to rescue a working relationship once you have made an accusation or shown bad feeling.

One final word of advice – once you have given the offending colleague the benefit of the doubt, do not subsequently complain about them to others – you do not want to be burdened with a reputation for being two-faced.

Step 3: Show some tolerance
Working with different people and their different personalities requires patience and understanding. There will be times when you want to scream at someone; tell them to get their act together; or shout at them to "Speed up!"

Restrain yourself. This sort of intolerance will not help your working relationships, and will certainly not facilitate the completion of the task in question. Take a deep breath. Calm down. Remember – the completion of tasks is not the only issue of importance at work.

Step 4: Always be a professional
Nothing causes more bad feeling than a colleague who fails in their promise to complete a piece of work, lets the team down by arriving late, doesn't pass on telephone messages, and so on.

Avoiding such behaviour, and remaining professional at all times will earn you respect and reduce any tension existing between you and a colleague.

3. Getting On – with Difficult Colleagues

Regardless of how professional, tolerant or thoughtful you are, you will inevitably encounter problems with some colleagues; you will, in these cases, find the following advice extremely valuable.

Problem 1: We Just Don't Get On
It happens.

Sometimes there is a 'clash of personalities': everything you do irritates them, and everything they do annoys you. You are either at each others' throats, or you are barely on speaking terms.

Don't panic.

Step 1: Think positive

Think about your colleague's positive qualities. What do you find most likeable about them? Think about your own attitude to the relationship. Are all your opinions justifiable? Are there any that could do with modifying? Think about the way you behave around your colleague. Praise them, pay them compliments – without being overly sycophantic – so that you are continually reminded of their positive characteristics.

Step 2: Talk, acknowledge, compromise

Bring the clash into the open by discussing it with your colleague. Acknowledge your different personalities; admit to each other what annoys you about the other, and why. Agree on some compromises: try to find some areas in which you are both prepared to change.

Step 3: Seek advice

If all else has failed, seek advice from a superior in an informal manner. Do not express your grievance in the form of a complaint against your colleague; present it, instead, as a difficulty with which you would like some help.

> **Golden Rule**
> The key to success is to get on with everyone *and* complete the task in hand.

Problem 2: They Are Constantly Late for Meetings

This is not always your problem, but if your colleague's lateness reflects on you, or results in you being kept waiting, it will become your problem.

Following the three-step plan below is better than suffering in silence, or – worse still – losing your temper and thus ruining the relationship.

Step 1: Acknowledge that it is a problem

Some people have no idea that their lack of punctuality is a problem. Explain how embarrassed you feel if you are meeting a client alone because your colleague is late, or because you are sitting on your own in a restaurant for 20 minutes.

Step 2: Acknowledge that it's not your problem

Try to avoid your colleague's lateness reflecting on anyone but themselves by not arranging to go anywhere with them where timeliness is of the essence, such as a meeting at another company.

Tell the colleague that you will join them at the location of the meeting so that, if they are late, at least you will have been punctual.

Step 3: Take action

Once you have attempted to deal with the problem, make it known that you will start any future meetings or appointments on time, with or without your colleague.

If they have not arrived for a business meeting, start without them.

If they are late for a lunch meeting, order your food without them.

Problem 3: They Criticise Me Constantly
"Your presentation was rather weak today, wasn't it?"
"I'm surprised to see you dressed like that for such an important meeting."

When colleagues are constantly criticising or putting you down, life can be very miserable indeed.

Step 1: Acknowledge the criticism
If ignoring the comments has no effect, try acknowledging the criticism instead. The trick is to echo the comment, showing that you are not prepared to ignore it and that you are inviting further explanation. If the comment is justified, you might get some valuable feedback. If not, your critic will usually back down.

> **Critic:** *"Your presentation was rather weak today, wasn't it?"*
> **Response:** *"You thought it was weak?"*

> **Critic:** *"I'm surprised to see you dressed like that for such an important meeting."*
> **Response:** *"You're surprised that I'm dressed like this?"*

Step 2: Clarify the criticism
Ask for further feedback. Separate the deserved from the undeserved criticism. Your colleague will be less likely to criticise, knowing that they will be challenged over every comment.

> **Critic:** *"Your presentation was rather weak today, wasn't it?"*
> **Response:** *"In what way?"*

> **Critic:** *"I'm surprised to see you dressed like that for such an important meeting."*
> **Response:** *"How is my dress inappropriate?"*

Step 3: Benefit from the criticism
Asking for the critic's help will give the appearance that you really value their comments thus endearing you to them and possibly avoiding any future (unnecessary) criticism. A request for help will also respond to the need for importance and power that these constant criticisms probably reflect.

> **Critic:** *"Your presentation was rather weak today, wasn't it?"*
> **Response:** *"Could you give me any tips? Perhaps when I give one next time, I can try it out on you first?"*

> **Critic:** *"I'm surprised to see you dressed like that for such an important meeting."*
> **Response:** *"What kind of thing do you think I should be wearing in this situation?"*

Golden Rule
Remember, constant criticism invariably says more about the (jealous or insecure) source of the comments than it does about you.

Problem 4: They Never Tell Me Anything

Such behaviour from a colleague is usually a sign that they are trying to establish power over you by withholding information.

Step 1: Acknowledge the overt problem

Go and see the colleague, saying that:

- you are concerned – you weren't informed about the matter in question.

- you would like to know if there was a reason for this.

Step 2: Acknowledge the covert problem

Ask if your not receiving information means that there is something else going on. Don't accuse; don't play the amateur psychologist. If they deny that there are any undercurrents, accept this.

Step 3: Keep them informed

If you keep your colleague informed about everything, it will:

- show them how you would like to be treated.

- make it hard for them to resist reciprocating.

Problem 5: They Keep Disturbing Me!

Your interpersonal skills have clearly paid off – this colleague likes you too much. They frequently stop by your desk for a 'quick' chat that interferes with your workflow. You feel awkward telling them that you are too busy to talk, so you end up desperately waiting for them to leave and then trying to pick up where you left off.

Step 1: Use some ground-rules

Stop by their desk one day, or chat over a coffee, and explain that sometimes you need to really concentrate on your work without any interruptions. Tell your colleague that you are always happy to talk to them during your break, or in quieter times, and reinforce this by stressing how much you get out of your chats.

Step 2: Use a sign

Agree with your colleague to use a sign indicating that you don't want to be disturbed. You could put a sign on your door; put a photograph the wrong way on your desk; or use a (polite!) hand signal on their approach.

Step 3: Use delaying tactics

If all else fails, smile and say:

> *"I'm so sorry but I have 15 minutes to finish this report. Could we meet for coffee later?"*

4. Getting On – with the Boss

The first step to getting on with your boss is to identify exactly what kind of boss they are.

The *Laissez-faire* Boss
Characteristics
- Very laid-back with a 'hands-off' approach to supervising.

- Places total trust in subordinates; maintains confidence in the ability of the staff.

- Rarely checks up on work or progress.

Suits
- Those who are self-motivated.

- Those who enjoy working on their own initiative.

Hints for handling the *Laissez-faire* Boss
- Be proactive. Arrange meetings or updates. The fact that your boss hasn't asked to see you doesn't mean that they don't want to.

- Keep the boss updated. Send memos, emails or reports regularly.

- Seek help if you need it. This type of boss is a good troubleshooter, and will expect you to come forward if there is a problem.

The Controlling Boss
Characteristics
- Wants to know continually what you are doing, how you are doing it and when it will be done.

- Frequently requests meetings, memos and reports.

Suits
- Those who are poor self-motivators.

- Those who lack self-confidence.

Hints for handling the Controlling Boss
- Update and inform them without being asked. Thus, if you are already self-motivated, it will show that you do not need close supervision.

- If you are unhappy or find yourself being too closely watched, suggest to your boss a try-out period of possibly a month with a more *laissez-faire* style.

The Aggressive Boss
Characteristics
- Bullies staff into complying with requests.

- Uses techniques such as shouting, disciplining in front of others, put-downs and sarcasm.

- Tends to criticise the individual rather than the behaviour.

- Very difficult to please.

Suits
- Few people – most will be demotivated by such aggression.

Hints for handling the Aggressive Boss
- Look through the aggression to the actual words spoken. If there is any truth in your boss's criticisms, demonstrate that you are working hard to improve.

- Try and talk quietly to your boss. Explain how their approach makes you feel.

- Avoid accusatory statements; instead say that this approach may work with some people, but not with you.
  Say:
  "That feels like a put-down and it's upsetting. Was that what you intended?"
  or:
  "That sounded sarcastic – did you mean it?"

The Empowering Boss
Characteristics
- Delegates well; gives you plenty of responsibility.

- Allows you to make decisions for yourself and decide your own work or project plans.

Suits
- The confident worker.

Hints for handling the Empowering Boss
- Check things out. If you are not sure that you are doing the right thing, confirm it with your boss.

- Be prepared to take risks.

- Have the courage of your convictions – your boss obviously thinks you are up to the task, and you should, too.

- Accept the responsibility. Don't be too afraid of the task. You may want to find someone else to double-check things with sometimes, so that you don't feel you are allowing your lack of confidence to filter through too much to your boss.

The Motivating Boss
Characteristics
- Generous with feedback and encouragement.

- Positive about your ideas and enthusiastic about your work.

Suits
- An enthused and creative employee.

Hints for handling the Motivating Boss

- Accept positive feedback. Some people find it hard to accept a compliment.

- Look for criticism, too. With this kind of boss, the negative feedback is often hidden behind the motivating elements, if they are afraid of demotivating you.

- Negative feedback, however, is just as important, so do look for it.

- Be creative. This is the ideal environment for coming up with ideas and plans; and your boss will like you the more for it.

The Demotivating Boss
Characteristics

- Negative about your work and ideas.

- Sees problems or downsides in everything you suggest.

Suits

- Only those with powerful self-motivation and the ability to ignore irrelevant criticism.

Hints for handling the Demotivating Boss

- Explain that you need positive feedback. Provide opportunities for this – if your boss mentions negative aspects in a report, point out the unmentioned areas and ask if they are all right.

- Be willing to improve. Ask to attend workshops or courses on the areas in which you receive criticism, if you believe that the criticism is deserved.

The Distant Boss
Characteristics

- Never available.

- Has too much to do or is simply not interested in your progress.

- Frequently fails to turn up for meetings or appointments.

Suits

- Organised individuals who work productively on their own. It shouldn't, however, have to suit anybody – your boss should be visible for at least part of the time.

Hints for handling the Distant Boss

- Keep a diary. Write down the times and events where you needed advice or input but were unable to obtain it.

- Arrange to meet your boss to discuss the problem. If they cancel, or fail to appear for three meetings, send a polite letter outlining the need to talk.

- Ask for another point of contact. Your own supervisor is clearly too busy.

5. Getting On – with Subordinates

Getting on with your subordinates is frequently the hardest part of any job and can be the source of many problems and frustrations for a supervisor.

Problem 1: They've Been There For Much Longer Than I Have

"I had been working as a trainee manager for one year when I was offered the post of branch manager at a branch that I had dealt with in my trainee capacity. I was 20 years old and without exception every staff member was older than me. Many had been there up to 20 years. So many changes were needed, but the staff all resented me and refused to listen to me. I could command no authority at all and when I called meetings, few even bothered to attend. It was so frustrating, but my own manager wasn't interested in my problems. I felt like a failure and I left after eight weeks."

Stephen, Managing Director

Step 1: Meet the employees
Meet with each individual employee on their own. Ask them how they feel about your position as manager. In such situations, when people are taken out and interviewed individually, they are more likely to be honest.

Step 2: If they say there's no problem
If they still cannot admit to having a problem, don't worry. It is much harder for individuals to behave badly if they have gone on record as saying they are happy with the situation.

Step 3: If they say there's a problem
If they do admit to having a problem, you now have a chance to try to put their minds at rest; or at least to acknowledge the issues.

Problem 2: They Are Always Late, or Spending Work Time on Personal Matters

Step 1: Do they know it's a problem?
Make the individual aware of the problem in an authoritative, but not confrontational, manner. Always give them the benefit of the doubt: never leap to instant conclusions about their behaviour.

Step 2: Are the phone calls still too frequent?
Explain that they are spending too long on personal calls, that such time eats into work productivity and that tying up the work lines costs the firm money. Ask them to limit phone calls to no more than one a day.

Step 3: Are the breaks still too long?
Ensure that you are visible at around the time when the breaks should end, to persuade employees back to work. At the end of the break, it is a good time to hand out new work or check on the progress of existing projects.

Problem 3: They Don't Recognise My Authority

"I was recently promoted, and ended up supervising ten workers. Eight were men, six were a lot older than me, and I had worked as peers with three of them. It was extremely difficult in the beginning, as they just didn't accept that I was their manager. They kept running to one of the other managers with their problems and concerns which made me look inadequate. If I asked them to do anything, they wouldn't comply unless they received orders from my male colleagues. In the end, I took each worker to one side and had a chat with them. I explained very firmly that I was their supervisor, which meant that my job was to supervise. I reminded them that my job also involved assessing them for promotion, but how could I give them positive appraisals when they kept running to other people? It was a veiled threat, but it seemed to work. It just reminded them of the real power I had."

Kate, Sales and Promotions Manager

Step 1: Be assertive

Project an image of self-confidence: learn to make requests or criticisms.

SEE CHAPTER 8

Step 2: Be authoritative

Wait for an occasion to demonstrate your authority, and make it clear that you are doing so.

Step 3: Be supported

If your authority is still in question, ask friendly colleagues or superiors to back you up.

Problem 4: They're Taking Advantage of Me

Some people will take advantage of the manager who doesn't continually check up on them. Few people work well in a completely liberal atmosphere: some guidelines and boundaries are often necessary.

Step 1: Get updates

Ask for regular monthly updates on the work in progress.

Step 2: Get evidence

Ask for appropriate evidence that work really is being done: reports, spreadsheets and so on.

Step 3: Get (reasonably) tough

If one worker still does not meet expectations, change your leadership style. Make sure, however, that you change your style with that worker alone. Other employees may come to resent an inexplicable and uncalled-for change in attitude.

Golden Rule

Work at developing good relationships with your subordinates; don't simply rely on discipline, or on forcing them continually to 'toe the line'.

A Note on Absenteeism

Problem: Employee frequently calls in sick

Step 1: Look at the worker's role
Workers who feel personally responsible for their work-load (through employee involvement and empowerment), or who know that others are relying on them, are less likely to take unnecessary absences than other employees. [Source: Mullins, 1996]

Step 2: Study the worker
Examine the employee's attitude to the work they are doing (assuming that they do not have genuine medical reasons for their absenteeism).

Step 3: Involve the worker
Try increasing their involvement at work, or giving them more power over their job and task design.

Caution
Workers are entitled to be off sick, and to suggest otherwise will not enhance your relationship with them.

6. Getting On – with Friends at Work

(Potential) Problem 1: The New Vacancy

"My friend was out of work. I felt so bad for her, when an opportunity arose in my customer service department, I recommended her in the highest possible terms to the boss. I genuinely thought she would be ideal... she had plenty of experience in customer service and she was great with people. I practically bullied my boss into giving her a go... he was happy to avoid having to advertise as we were only a small firm. I was delighted when she got it. I imagined all those great gossips we would have, and the support we'd give each other. Unfortunately, things didn't work out too well. To start with, she began arriving late, asking me to cover for her. It was really embarrassing as I hated lying, but she was my best friend, so what could I do? Then she started skiving – asking me to say she was sick when she just fancied a day off. I got really annoyed with her – it is my reputation on the line too! In fact, I stood to lose a great deal. How would my boss ever trust me again if he thought I could recommend such a poor worker? What kind of judgement would he think I had? This would really raise questions about my management potential... I had been angling for promotion, but now seriously doubted I would get it."

Helena, Promotions Manager

Be cautious about recommending your friends for positions within your company. Refrain from pushing your boss into employing your friends and do not automatically give them a glowing reference.

If you are asked for your view, say that you only know them socially and could not comment on their work abilities. That way, if things go horribly wrong, you won't end up taking the blame.

(Potential) Problem 2: I've Been Promoted

"I worked with Kath for three years and we were really friendly. We went out together at weekends, and even holidayed together one year. Then I got promoted. It was brilliant – I was so pleased, but Kath wasn't. She said it would be the end of our friendship, but I assured her things would stay the same, even though I was now, technically, her superior. But things didn't stay the same. I found it really hard asking her to do things, and she became resentful and awkward. She was preventing me from doing my job properly. I stopped joining her in the canteen – it was just impossible to be her equal in the café, but then tell her what to do ten minutes later. When I got promoted I lost a best friend – but also, my job became a nightmare, thanks to her."

Melanie, Account Manager

Try not to become too close with people at work; make sure you have a healthy social life outside the office and the people in it. That way you won't be left feeling awkward (and friendless) in the event of a promotion – yours or theirs.

If you or they are promoted, sit down together and acknowledge that things will be different from now on. Devise some groundrules which dictate how you should both now behave in and out of the office.

Agree, possibly, to see less of each other at work. Perhaps you will have to cut down on social activities, but there is no reason to cut them all out. Agree also that the un-promoted friend will allow the promoted one to do their job, which may mean following the orders of the latter.

(Potential) Problem 3: It's Too Cliquey

Not everybody will find your relationship with your friend as rewarding as you do. Cliques and cliquey behaviour make the rest of the office feel isolated and irritated; you are also suggesting that your friend matters more than anybody else.

- Don't share private jokes with your friend – if you must, always explain the joke to listeners.

- Avoid spending tea and coffee breaks, or lunches, exclusively with your friend. Invite others to join you.

- Don't do favours for your friend that you wouldn't do for anyone else in the office.

7. Getting On – with Customers or Clients

Customers or clients can be demanding, aggressive, angry, and even abusive. Since most companies emphasise that 'the customer is always right', it can be extremely difficult for many employees to remain calm in the face of such provocation.

Problem 1: The Customer is Angry

Why is the customer angry?

There is usually only one reason for the customer to be angry, and that is as a result of poor quality service. The most common customer grievances, listed below, all stem from poor quality service.

- *"I can't get through."* The lines are constantly engaged; the numbers are not widely available; the customer is put on hold repeatedly; or re-routed several times.

- *"No one's taking this seriously."* The customer feels that their complaint is simply not being responded to or cared about. The responses, *"We'll get back to you,"* (and subsequently not doing so) or, *"There's nothing we can do,"* are simply not adequate in any way.

- *"They've done it again!"* Having to put up with repeated mistakes.

- *"No one's told us anything."* There are few things worse for a customer than lack of information such as not being told the reason for the delay, fault or problem.

Dealing with the angry customer

Step 1: Acknowledge, sympathise, apologise
- Acknowledge. Show that you hear and feel their anger. They will be doing all they can to display their displeasure: the sooner you acknowledge it, the sooner they can stop displaying it.

- Sympathise. Say:
  "You must feel so angry [disappointed/let down]."

- Apologise. Say:
  "I'm so sorry you have been put to this trouble."
  or:
  "I'm so sorry that you have had problems."

Step 2: Understand the problem
Make sure that you understand the problem and have all the facts. Sympathise with the treatment they have received. It may even be appropriate for you to express outrage at what the customer has experienced.

Step 3: Deal with the problem
Devise a clear strategy to right the wrong that the customer feels. Make sure that the customer knows what will happen, and that their complaint is being taken seriously.

Generally speaking, customers will tolerate almost any problem with a product as long as the service, or aftercare, is good.

Ask the customer if they are satisfied with the solution you are offering. If they are not satisfied, either come up with another solution, or speak to your supervisor.

A customer boarded the plane and proceeded to vent his anger at the flight attendant because he had requested a window seat on each of his six recent flights with this airline; and on each occasion had been told that his request had been accepted – only to find each time that the seat he had been assigned was an aisle seat.

The flight attendant responded immediately with:

"That's terrible! You must be feeling furious – how can that have happened? I know I wouldn't be pleased if that happened to me."

The customer's anger visibly drained from his face.

Problem 2: The Customer is Abusive

Step 1: Remember your rights

Remember that you have rights. Everyone has the right not to be abused at work, and you do not have to put up with it.

Step 2: Talk to the customer

Attempt first to disarm the customer with some of the techniques outlined above. If they remain abusive, ask the customer what it is they want you to do. That may stop the flow of abuse and make them consider what they really do want.

Step 3: Hang up or leave

Failing all this, simply tell them that you feel they are being abusive, and that you have been told that you do not have to deal with abusive customers. Give them advance warning; then leave, or put the phone down.

Problem 3: The Customer Talks for Hours

The customer who won't get off the phone is often lonely, and enjoys having someone to listen. Don't feel too guilty about putting them off – at the end of the day, you have your job to do.

Step 1: Interrupt

Wait for them to take a breath, or for a suitable break in their story. Apologise for interrupting.

Step 2: Invent a more pressing demand

After you have apologised for interrupting, explain that the other line is ringing; that you are being summoned by your supervisor; even that the fire alarm has gone off.

Step 3: Get to the real reason for their call

Ask them if there is anything you can do for them quickly, before you rush off. If they launch back into a long speech, repeat the process from Step 1.

Chapter Checkpoint

After reading this chapter, you should:

- know how to deal with the main four character types.

- have learnt the essentials for how to get along with colleagues.

- know how to cope with 'problem' colleagues.

- have discovered the seven varieties of boss, and how to deal with each one.

- know how to deal with subordinates.

- be aware of the pitfalls of working with friends

- know the problems of, and the solutions for, dealing with customers

In the Next Chapter

Teamwork — how to work in a team, and profit from the experience.

Further Reading

Sutherland, V., and C. L. Cooper, *30 Minutes to Deal with Difficult People* (London: Kogan Page, 1997).

Cava, R., *Dealing with Difficult People: Power Strategies for Handling Stressful Situations* (London: Piatkus, 1990).

Bramson, R. M., *Coping with Difficult Bosses* (London: Nicholas Brealey Publishing, 1993).

Chapter Four

In It Together: The Art of Teamwork

The Aim

Career advancement – a great team player has a great future.

Today, few people work in isolation; most people are part of at least one team, and many are part of several.

It is safe to say that the team will permeate almost every area of your working life. To get on and succeed in the workplace you must know how to function well within a group, and how to deal with the many issues that teamwork presents.

Before you can hone your teamworking skills, you must first understand exactly what a team is and what constitutes its different characteristics. Having established that you can subsequently move on to the more complex area of team growth and identify the four vital stages of team development.

Teams are not autonomous structures, however, and it cannot be forgotten that a team comprises different individuals, with different ideas, beliefs and goals. It is necessary to thoroughly understand the various roles that exist in the group, who adopts them, and why; this includes yourself.

There is no doubt that, once a team is properly established, it frequently thinks – or tries to – with one mind, unanimous on every decision. Although on one hand productive, such behaviour inevitably leads to problems where the pressure of conforming is concerned; difficulties that you must know how to tackle if you are to work successfully with others. Of course, such problems are not alone in making teamwork often stressful and frustrating: learning to cope with a myriad of other obstacles will clear the way for you to become a successful team player, part of a successful and progressive team. It can only help your career.

1. The Team – What Is It?

James is a marketing assistant for a large national company. Marketing assistants tend to be assigned to help on several campaigns at once and each campaign has a team consisting of a marketing manager, a couple of assistants, plus various members from other departments, such as advertising. James is currently involved in three campaigns and is thus a member of three different teams. In addition, there are seven marketing assistants in the company and he feels that he is part of a group with them; they are often sent on training programmes together for instance. He also plays in the work football team and is part of a group lottery syndicate.

A team can be defined as: *a number of individuals who rely on each other to solve problems, achieve tasks, or gain information.*

James is a member of six different teams. In James's office, as in all work environments, some of these teams are formally established while others are more informal groupings that evolve over time.

All teams and groups can be identified by certain characteristics. In the main, these two terms are interchangeable; however, in certain respects (see the point on 'Reliance', below) 'teams' and 'groups' can become two very distinct concepts.

Team Characteristics – Identification
Those who are members of a group are clearly distinguishable from those who aren't.

Example:
James and the other lottery members are clearly parts of the syndicate whilst everyone else is not.

Team Characteristics – Recognition
A collection of individuals are all fans of a particular film star. They remain diverse individuals until such time as they join a fan-club – when, subsequently, they recognise each other as fans, and members of the club, and thus become a group in the true sense of the word.

The members of a group must recognise that they are part of that group. A selection of individuals may share common goals and purposes, but unless they recognise each other they are not a group at all.

Team Characteristics – A Shared Purpose
However diverse they may be as individuals, the members must have a common goal or shared interest. What makes this a group is the common purpose that the members have for being in the group.

Example:
In the case of James, football is the shared purpose of one group while a marketing campaign is the common interest of another.

Team Characteristics – Interaction
The members of the group interact or communicate; they influence one another and react accordingly. The interaction may be face-to-face or, in the case of computer user-groups, occurs without members even meeting.

Team Characteristics – Reliance
The group becomes a team when the members are reliant on each other for skills, knowledge and advice.

Team Characteristics – Shared Values
Finally, the group members share common norms or values that regulate their behaviour (see the note on norms, below).

2. The Team – How It Grows

All groups pass through several distinct phases. What distinguishes a team is the conscious attempt to push a group through the same stages, but in a more structured way.

Thus the four stages of team development, as identified by social psychologist B. W. Tuckman, are 'Forming'; 'Storming'; 'Norming'; and 'Performing'. [Source: Tuckman, 1965]

The Stages

Each of the four stages is unique; each one is characterised by different types of behaviour and varying issues.

Understanding these stages and their impact upon the team will enable you to deal successfully with the problems that arise during the various phases of team development.

Stage 1: Forming

This forming stage may happen several times in the life of the team, as members and managers move to new jobs or new companies.

Forming behaviour

The various members of the group will be asking themselves a series of questions to which they need answers before they can take any risks or show any initiative. Such questions will typically include:

- what is this team supposed to do?
- how can I contribute?
- will my views be valued?
- am I only meant to speak when asked?
- will the loudest voice be heard?
- will I be able to say what I really think?
- will I have to attend every meeting?
- will I have a lot of work to do?

Such questions usually result in the following behaviour:

- people will be polite and formal, as they try their best to fit in and be accepted.
- they will be keeping ideas and thoughts simple.
- they will be trying to avoid sensitive or controversial topics or ideas.
- they will avoid disclosing too much personal information.
- they will avoid criticising other team members wherever possible.

Potential Forming problems

- A common goal cannot be agreed upon.

- The team does not wish to discuss aims and objectives.

- Cliques are forming.

- Some members feel frustrated by the slow speed of the decision-making process.

Golden Rule
Remember – it is quite natural to feel anxious and confused during this stage of the process as difficulties and uncertainties are ironed out.

Stage 2: Storming
This is a tough stage, characterised by competition and conflict. Such behaviour is to be expected; in fact, it is not only normal but necessary if the group is to eventually function productively.

Storming behaviour
In this second stage, the behaviour of the team will be geared towards assertion, in order for individuals to gain influence and identity.

- The leader, or figure of authority, is likely to be challenged.

- People will start to express their own views more forcibly.

- They may challenge the ideas of others.

- There may be evidence of poor listening.

- There may be a lot of defensive behaviours.

- Emotions such as anger may be expressed more freely.

- Some team members may withdraw entirely and stay silent.

Potential Storming problems

- People might be talking loudly and aggressively.

- Other people stay silent and subdued.

- Some members think that the group is wasting time.

- Certain individuals believe that they could achieve more by working alone.

- Disillusionment, or perhaps a reaction against an over-dominant team member, leads to a potentially-successful group disbanding.

Conflict between members should not necessarily be discouraged. Attempts to resolve disagreement through compromise or majority rule will only mean that views are suppressed rather than resolved; and the Storming stage will not be fully worked through.

Golden Rule
Difficulties during the Storming stage are part of the whole 'teething' process of forming a successful team, and in no way impede the chances of the group becoming fully productive.

Stage 3: Norming
During Norming, the conflict of the Storming stage begins to be resolved and is replaced instead by co-operation and collaboration.

At this point, a group identity should be emerging, and this new collective identity will subsequently bind the team together.

Norms: a set of shared values, or ways of behaving, which often act as guidelines for group members.

Norms create expectations about which behaviours will be tolerated, and which will not. They dictate the rules governing a variety of areas for teams, including:

- the type of language used – swearing, jovial, politically correct, and so on.
- the tone of voice used – aggressive, perhaps, or cold.
- the clothes worn – smart, casual, power-dressing...
- the working methods – maybe everyone takes notes, or prepares reports for meetings, and so on.
- role conflict – as individuals start to assume their respective roles within the teams.

Norming behaviour
- Open exchanges of ideas.
- An increased receptiveness to others' thoughts, and a willingness to change one's own, preconceived, ideas.
- A developing respect for leadership.
- Active participation by all in group discussions or activities.
- A high level of creativity.
- Acceptance by all of the group norms.

Potential Norming problems
- Role conflict, as individuals start to assume their respective roles within the teams.

Stage 4: Performing

By now there is a highly developed group identity: members feel loyalty towards the group, and towards the other members.

At this stage, the cohesion in the group may well make it difficult for newcomers to break in.

Performing behaviour

- A sense of openness and trust.

- Strong relationships between members.

- An easy acceptance of differences by the group and its members.

- An increasingly willing acceptance of roles.

- No difficulties in assigning tasks to individuals.

- A high level of productivity.

3. The Team – Who Is It?

During the two final stages of team development, Norming and Performing, members start – formally or informally – to take on certain roles. The word 'role' serves here as a theatrical metaphor: in other words, the part that a worker performs in the workplace team.

Within any team exists a variety of roles that members can slip into at relevant times and subsequently drop once out of the team. Team roles are specific to the group situation and can be completely independent of your other roles in life.

> **Example:**
> Manager at work – has Supervisor, Teacher and Counsellor roles.
> Manager at home – instantly becomes partner, father or mother, or may adopt a different role to their team role at work, becoming instead a Devil's Advocate amongst friends.

Depending on the personality of the other team members, and the nature of the team, it is possible to take on many different roles within different group situations.

The Ideal Roles?

Psychologists and organisational consultants have devoted much time to stipulating which roles should be adopted for optimal team productiveness ('Evaluator'; 'Implementer'; and so on).

It is more likely, however, that most teams will not adopt these 'ideal' roles. Instead, the personality characteristics of members or of the group generally will give rise to a variety of roles which won't necessarily further the team's progress. In some cases, these unofficial group roles will actually hinder the aims of the team.

The group does not necessarily need nine individuals, because some members will invariably take on more than one role. Team-building exercises, designed to focus the energies of the group, are often concentrated upon dividing the nine roles within the group, thus ensuring that the team operates at the greatest possible level of productiveness. **[Source Belbin, 1981 and 1993]**

What are the Real Roles?

If you can identify what the informal roles of your team are, you are one step closer to dealing with team difficulties that arise from these roles, or from role conflict (which occurs when people are uncomfortable with the role they have).

The following self-assessment quiz will enable you to define firstly your own role; and subsequently, if necessary, the roles of the other team-members.

R. M. Belbin identified nine roles that he felt team members needed to fulfil in order for the team to be successful. These included:

- the 'Plant' – the source of new ideas.

- the 'Evaluator' – monitors and evaluates these ideas.

- the 'Implementer' – organises the practicalities of the ideas.

- the 'Team Worker' – aims to keep the team working together.

- the 'Resource Investigator' – obtains information from outside the group.

- the 'Technical Specialist' – is responsible for the specialist knowledge that the group needs.

What is my Role?

Ask yourself the following questions – if your answer is 'Yes', make a note of the corresponding letter.

Do I tend to get irritated if the group discusses matters not directly related to the problem in hand?	A
Do I tend to speak more than others in the group?	J
Am I reluctant to make, and stand by, decisions?	E
Do I tend to start my sentences with 'I'?	G
Do I generally think that rules are there for a reason?	B
Do I ask other people for their views?	H
Do I tend to ask for more information?	E
Am I often convinced that the task cannot be achieved?	K
Do I feel that the group goals are not really of interest to me?	F
Do I think rules are there to be broken?	C
Do I interrupt a lot?	J
Do I get impatient with all the group discussion?	I
Do I rarely listen to other opinions?	G
Do I like initiating things more than following them through?	D
Am I always pointing out the rules, or how things ought to be done?	B
Do I enjoy finding a way to get round the rules?	C
Do I frequently dismiss ideas or suggestions because they 'won't work'?	K
Do I worry about the quieter members of the group?	H
Do I often repeat what people have said in order to clarify it?	A
Do I really care what people feel as long as the right decision is made?	I
Do I feel that I have better things to do than be part of this group?	F
Do I frequently suggest solutions?	D
Do I feel uncomfortable if the group may be doing things the wrong way?	B
Do I get very impatient with red tape and rules?	C
Do I tend to see the faults in everything?	K
Do I like facts and figures more than thoughts or opinions?	E
Do I tend to plant a lot of ideas in the group that lead to new discussions?	D
Do I think it is important for everyone to be happy with group decisions?	H
Am I concerned if the group goes off at a tangent?	A
Do I feel that the group could manage very well without me?	F
Do I think I am usually right?	G
Do I think that the result is more important than how we get there?	I
Do I feel uncomfortable if I am not the leader?	J

Mostly As: Focusser

- Defines the goals.

- Summarises what has happened.

- Points out if the discussions have strayed from their intended purpose.

- Can be relied upon to bring the group's attention back to the matter in hand.

Mostly Bs: Bureaucrat

- Continually states how things ought to be done.

- Points out what the rules are.

- Is reluctant to allow the group to avoid the rules or even to be unaware of them.

Mostly Cs: Non-conformer

- Tries to ignore the rules or knows ways of getting round them.

- Hates bureaucracy and red tape.

- Gets very impatient with the Bureaucrat.

Mostly Ds: Ideas Person

- Suggests new ideas to the group.

- Brings new group aims or goals to the team.

- Thinks of new procedures or new solutions.

- Generally allows the group to evolve in new directions.

Mostly Es: Fact-seeker

- Needs clarification in terms of factual accuracy.

- Seeks information and facts relevant to the problem.

- Reluctant to accept information or ideas on face value.

- Very cautious and careful.

Mostly Fs: Uninvolved

- Not emotionally engaged in the team.

- Present out of obligation alone.

- Does not feel involved or responsible; thus does not participate much.

Mostly Gs: Opinionated

- Continually gives an opinion, rather than objective views or ideas.

- Does not encourage the opinions of other people.

Mostly Hs: Peacemaker

- Concerned with how the task is achieved, and with everyone being happy and comfortable.

- Seeks opinions.

- Tries to pull the group together, and co-ordinate it.

- Mediates between people.

- Gives praise.

Mostly Is: Task Achiever
- Concerned only that the task is achieved.

- Pushes the group to take action and make decisions.

- Frequently ignores the views and opinions of others.

Mostly Js: Dominator
- Tries to assert authority or superiority by dominating all conversations.

- Attempts to exclude others.

Mostly Ks: Devil's Advocate
- Frequently finds fault with ideas and plans.

- Critical and negative.

- Gives the impression of being a pessimist and doom-monger.

> **Note**
> With such a short questionnaire, it is quite possible that no one single role will emerge; additionally, many of us play a mixture of several different roles.

Roles and their Problems

Problem 1: The Dominators are dominating

Step 1: Explain the roles
Use the quiz above to determine the roles of each individual, and explain the different roles to your team. Suggest that the group assign formal group roles to members. Make sure that people are taking roles they would not otherwise adopt – for example, encourage the Dominator to take the role of the Peacemaker.

Step 2: Reassess the situation
Open team discussions again; interrupting the Dominator whenever necessary. Take note: if you take on the role of Peacemaker yourself in this situation, you will subsequently be able to encourage others to contribute.

Step 3: Split the group
If Steps 1 and 2 have not yet worked, split the group up. The aim should be to put the quieter people in a different group to the Dominators – to allow them at least an opportunity to contribute.

Problem 2: Role-conflict – I'm not happy with my role

The most frequently-unhappy people are those who have found themselves becoming Devil's Advocate, or Fact-Seeker. At first the role may seem natural to them, but after a while they want to grow and develop with the rest of the team and find this impeded by their ascribed role.

Step 1: Explain the roles (again)

Bring the whole issue of roles to the top of your group agenda, and explain role theory to the rest of the team. Suggest that each member identify which role they have, and subsequently ensure that everybody actively takes on a different role.

Step 2: Take a fresh look

With your new role, not only do you no longer have to be Devil's Advocate, but you should also use the opportunity to see into the minds of other members. By adopting somebody else's role, and standing in their shoes, you will be better able to see why they have the viewpoints they have or make the decisions that they make.

Step 3: Keep it up!

Even if the team eventually switches back to the old roles, make sure that you all continue to use the greater understanding that you have gained.

4. The Team – How the Team Thinks

The team is a double-edged sword. A group of people can pool skills, resources, information and knowledge; share different viewpoints and perspectives and generate an extremely high output. On the other hand, working in a team necessitates a loss, to a degree, of individuality; and produces some interesting interaction between the members.

Not all this interaction is positive; in fact, some can be seriously detrimental to the group, the group members and the decisions made by the group, and should be guarded against. The two most frequently-recurring problems arising from team-thinking processes are 'Conformity' and 'Groupthink', and they are potential minefields of which you must be aware.

The Sheep Syndrome – Conformity

"I was lecturing to a group of 250 first-year university students. The topic, although they didn't know it, was conformity, and I decided to perform an experiment. I simply asked everyone to stand on their seat and put their hands on their head. I was interested to see what the reactions would be. Would they comply with my request? Would they just laugh? For about a minute nothing happened. Faces stared blankly at me, waiting to see if I would give them a clue as to how to behave. I just repeated the request with a solemn face. Finally, one person stood on his chair a little hesitantly, waiting for my reaction. I just nodded to him. Then people started following him, one by one at first, then in tens and twenties. Within three minutes all 250 of them were standing on their chairs with their hands on their heads."

Jane, Lecturer

Conformity can come about as a result of the pressure that groups exert to get members to agree with them. When groups form, a 'herd instinct' compels people to follow the crowd, even if they disagree with the crowd. Why?

What Makes People Conform?

A need to be correct
When we are uncertain about what to do, we look towards others to see how they are behaving. If the majority of them are behaving in a certain way, then we feel that they must be right and, like sheep, we follow.

We want to be liked and accepted
Even if we know that the herd is wrong, we may – against our better judgement – follow, simply in order to fit in.
[Source: Deutsch and Garrard, 1955]

The Advantages – and Disadvantages – of Conformity

Advantages
* Conformity helps us behave in socially acceptable ways.

* Conformity helps us decide what to do if we are uncertain.

Disadvantages
* Conformity can result in groupthink, which should be avoided (see the section on 'Groupthink', below).

[Source: Deutsch and Garrard, 1955]

In order to reduce the effects of conformity within groups, we need to look at what factors or attributes of groups are likely to result in pressure on you to conform.

What Will Prevent Conformity?

The size of the group
If there are two people and you both disagree, conformity is low; it's just their word against yours. With a larger group, of course, if you are in a minority of one the pressure to conform is much greater.

Introducing another dissenter
If another member of the group agrees with you and disagrees with the majority, the pressure to conform is significantly reduced.

Having a Devil's Advocate is thus a good idea – it automatically decreases the tendency towards conformity.

How dissenters are treated
Dissenters are often treated with ridicule and derision. By introducing rules which disallow laughing or ridicule, the risk of conformity is again reduced.

How decisions are taken
Dissenters are often reluctant to speak out in public. A private vote that allows anonymity will reduce pressure to conform.

I'm in the Minority – How Can I Resist Conforming?
There may well be times when you are convinced that you are right, and that everyone else is wrong. There is nothing, however, which says that the minority cannot influence the majority – it is entirely possible for your lone voice not only to be heard, but also to be acted-upon.

Max, an independent training consultant, was working in a team of five on developing a training package. The rest of the group wanted to develop a package on presentation skills for managers. Max was convinced that the market for such a package was saturated and that it would be far more lucrative to develop a leadership training package. He was outvoted, but because he wasn't happy, the others agreed to give him a couple of weeks to 'prove' his case.

Max spent the next two weeks working long hours developing marketing questionnaires and taking it to a sample of managers. The questionnaire asked them which kind of training package they would be more likely to attend. The extra work meant that he even worked weekends and missed a football match he had tickets for. He gave the tickets to another member of the group who supported the same team (he was thus able to demonstrate how like the other he was in every other way). Finally, he made his presentation of the results which did point convincingly to the leadership course. However, he did also offer to run a smaller course in presentation skills alongside and his plans were accepted by the others in the team.

> **With persistence, and backed by inevitable cultural change, it is quite possible for the minority to become the majority – after all, in the last century, those with anti-racist views were in the minority.**

The three-step plan that Max followed is explained below.

Step 1: Hold fast to your views
The best way to influence the majority is to steadfastly maintain your view. Ensure, therefore, that your view is correct – there is no point clinging stubbornly to flawed or invalid views.

Be wary, however, of being too inflexible. You will make a greater impact on others if you agree to some compromise and you will not then be dismissed as a radical or an extremist.

Step 2: Be principled, be dedicated
Always be seen as acting out of principle for what you believe to be right, rather than because someone else is pulling your strings. A principled individual will be prepared to make a sacrifice. Indeed, if you are seen to be making a personal or material sacrifice for what you believe is right, the others are likely to take your view more seriously.

Principles exert influence. We are more convinced by a famous person endorsing an unpopular campaign if they are not being paid, than if they are. Consider Diana, Princess of Wales, who turned AIDS from a minority cause into a popular one.

Step 3: Find some common ground
You will have greater influence if you appear to be similar to the majority in every way (except, of course, with regard to the conflicting view). People are more likely to listen to those who are like themselves.
[Source: Moscovici, 1976]

If conformity remains unchecked, the result is usually extremely detrimental to the decision-making processes of the group and results in a condition known as 'group-think'.

'Groupthink'
Ten members of a pharmaceutical company are meeting to discuss the launch of a new product that they have spent two years researching. It is a crisis meeting called by the CEO of the company, who has heard that a similar product is being researched by a rival company and could be on the market within six months. The original plan had been to launch the product within four months, but now the team needs to decide whether to launch earlier in order to secure the market share before their rivals get in on the act. The team has been working together on the product for well over two years and has been meeting regularly throughout that time. They know each other very well; they laugh, joke, and sometimes even socialise with each other.

When they meet, the CEO immediately starts by saying that they must bring the launch forward. One member, Jo, shifts uncomfortably in his chair, and then ventures to speak. He points out that the initial trials of the product suggest that although it has been considered safe enough to meet the government regulations, new findings were coming in to suggest that it may not be as safe as they first thought.

The CEO asks Jo, simply, "Does it meet safety standards?" to which Jo reluctantly replies that it does.

"Right, any other objections to pressing ahead with the launch?" demands the CEO, sweeping Jo's objection aside. No other objections are stated and the product is launched. It is several years before the team realises that the safety aspect was not as rigorous as it could have been, and the company ends up with several lawsuits that result in bankruptcy.

Above scenario based on a real-life situation

What is Groupthink?
In 1972, an influential theorist called Janis analysed a number of American foreign policy decisions made between 1940 and 1970. He came to the conclusion that the decision-making processes in each case were flawed as a result of what he termed 'groupthink'. [Source: Janis, 1972]

What Causes Groupthink?

Cohesion
The group making the decisions has a strong identity, and bonds of loyalty towards each member are strong, too.

Isolation
This may refer to literal isolation, but may also be psychological isolation so that members discard outside influences or information.

Premature consensus
The group members fail to search systematically for alternative solutions before selecting the way forward. They reach consensus too early, and any disagreement is discouraged.

Stress
The group is often under pressure to reach a conclusion as quickly as possible because of time or external factors.

A strong leader
The group is led by a particularly controlling or authoritative individual.

What are the Symptoms of Groupthink?

Discouragement of dissenters
A very cohesive group is likely to exert pressure on dissenters to conform to the majority view. Some of this pressure is implicit or hidden, but often people who disagree will feel that they may be fired or sacked if they do not toe the line.

An illusion of unanimity
Because everyone finally toes the line, the group feels itself to be unanimous, believing that the decision must be the correct one because everyone agrees with it.

An illusion of invulnerability
The group acts with excessive optimism and takes high risks, convinced that they are both correct and invincible.

Strategies to Avoid Groupthink
The leader should adopt a neutral role, and should avoid stating their preferences too early in the process. They should subsequently encourage the minority view, in order that a wider variety of options can be considered.

An official Devil's Advocate should be introduced at this stage; it is their job to actually seek out opposing views or to find information to suggest that the accepted view is wrong. [Source: Janis, 1972]

5. The Team – the Problems

Problem 1: Everyone Has a Different Agenda

A team is meeting to decide how to divide the tasks required by a new project. This is the open agenda and has been confirmed in a written memo to all the team members. However, each of the individual members comes to the meeting with another hidden and personal agenda.

For David, it is whether he will be able to get the role he has been angling for.

For Louisa it is fear that her preferred task will be taken away from her.

Seamus is concerned that his skills will not be recognised.

Karen is just worried that she will have yet another task to deal with when she cannot cope with the workload she has.

Thus, as the open agenda is being worked through, each member is not working on a group goal. Instead they are all working in their own individual interests.

Hidden agendas can really disrupt the working of the group, since the team is no longer a cohesive unit working with one goal.

Solution

Gently question individuals, and persuade them to reveal their hidden agendas. Suggest at the same time that it is perfectly normal for team members to have fears and concerns.

Problem 2: There is conflict between two or more members

Conflict and disagreement is a normal part of Storming. It should not be suppressed and should in fact be encouraged: putting forward different views and opinions will usually produce the best decisions. There are ways of making conflict productive or, if things have gone too far, of reconciling varying viewpoints.

Step 1: Deal with the emotion

Remember that conflict can make people emotional and personally offended. Ask the conflicting parties how they feel, and encourage them to express their feelings without resorting to emotional outbursts.

Step 2: Summarise, examine, and test the viewpoints

- Summarise and clarify the different viewpoints, encouraging each person to really listen to the views of others.

- Examine how far apart the two views actually are. Sometimes the difference in opinions can be smaller than it seems.

- Test how much the difference in opinion really matters. Ask each party how important the issue is to them, on a scale of 1–100. Often one or both will realise that it is a trivial point after all, but one that has been blown out of proportion.

Step 3: Can it be resolved?
If not, agree on a course of action such as later discussion, gathering of more information or taking on board some outside views.

Problem 3: Nobody Listens to Me!
It is common for some people to feel that their views are not being taken seriously by the team; that they do not have the confidence to voice their ideas; or that someone else is preventing them from speaking out. The individual feels inadequate and disenchanted and, in the worst-case scenario, leaves the group.

Step 1: Speak up
Bring the issue out into the open in a non-threatening way. Ask for a moment to speak at the start or end of a meeting and explain your feelings.

Step 2: Don't point the finger
Avoid blaming either an individual, the group as a whole or 'some people' in the group. Simply state the problem as you see it and as you feel it. Invite others to respond with the view from over there. It's possible that they will sympathise with you, or even admit that they were at fault.

Step 3: Move on
Suggest ways in which you and the team can move on. Ask that a new rule be implemented which will discourage interrupting and encourage turn-taking.

Problem 4: The Others are Letting us Down
Problems often arise when team members:

- come late to meetings.

- don't come to meetings at all.

- don't do what was expected.

- aren't prepared.

- chat noisily throughout meetings.

- fail to meet obligations.

Step 1: Consider the situation
Make sure that you examine the reasons for such behaviour from team members. Are they feeling excluded, or alienated?

Step 2: Address the situation
Using the information you have gleaned so far in this chapter, try to address any issues raised in Step 1, above.

Step 3: Establish a constitution
Once you have dealt with any other unresolved issues, the way to combat unreliability is to form a constitution, and to establish thereby a set of rules.

The Constitution could be as follows:

Rule 1: We will all be on time for meetings; and meetings will start promptly.

Rule 2: If we cannot attend the meeting, we will inform the team leader in advance – preferably at least one day in advance.

Rule 3: We will meet any obligations agreed to in previous meetings.

Rule 4: We will come to meetings prepared for the agenda, and with any information that will be required at hand.

Rule 5: We will respect other people by listening to them when they speak.

Problem 5: One Person is Forever Blocking Ideas

Just one person's negativity can affect the entire team. It is important to use strategies from preventing the Devil's Advocate from entirely blocking creativity and decision-making processes.

Step 1: Have a positive attitude
Don't say: *"We've already tried that and it didn't work."*
Say: *"Well, we did try that but we could try again."*

Don't say: *"That will cost too much."*
Say: *"Can we do that within the budget?"*

Don't say: *"No one will buy it."*
Say: *"Will people buy it?"*

Don't say: *"You're not serious, are you?"*
Say: *"Are you submitting this as a proposal?"*

Don't say: *"Have you really thought that through?"*
Say: *"Have you done the research on this?"*

Step 2: Have a brainstorm!
The brainstorm can serve as an opportunity for everyone in the group to suggest ideas that can be wacky or wild. Only one rule should apply – no one is allowed to comment or to criticise anyone's ideas.

Use a flipchart to write the ideas down as they trip off people's tongues. At the end, each idea has to be considered carefully.

Step 3: Have a look at advantages vs. disadvantages
Consider each idea in terms of its benefits and costs. Ensure that the team comes up with positive aspects to each idea. This will prevent excessive negativity.

Emotions are contagious – we 'catch' them from other people. [Source: Hatfield, Cacioppo and Rapson, 1992] If one person sends out negativity, just watch the rest of the team slump into despair. We tend to mimic other peoples' emotional expressions as though they were 'a kind of social virus' – hence the effectiveness of advertising in which smiling models are used; or why 'canned laughter' is frequently used in mediocre sit-coms. [Source: Goleman, 1996]

Problem 6: We're 'Performing' – But We Have A New Member
When a team or group has successfully moved through each of the four stages, it can be extremely frustrating to have a new member join. This person will have new ideas, new ways of thinking, will not know the group norms, how to behave, what is expected, or what the goals are. There is a danger that this person can disrupt the group by forcing them back to earlier stages.

Step 1: Tell them the rules
The solution is to integrate the newcomer into the group carefully; make sure that, before joining the team, the member is thoroughly briefed and oriented about the values, goals, norms, expectations and rules.

Step 2: Tell them what's been done
Give the newcomer a history of the group. If possible, share the minutes of meetings with them.

Step 3: Find a mentor
Assign an experienced member of the team to act as a mentor, and ease the new member into a role within the group.

Chapter Checkpoint

After reading this chapter, you should:

- know what a team is.

- understand what the four stages of development of a team are.

- know about team roles, and have identified yours.

- understand conformity and groupthink and how to avoid them.

- have explored typical team problems, and how to overcome them.

In the Next Chapter

Gossip, politics and power in the workplace – you can't avoid them but you can profit from them!

Further Reading

Syer, J. D., *How Teamwork Works: The Dynamics of Effective Team Development* (London: McGraw-Hill, 1996).

Scott, K., *Teams, Teamwork and Teambuilding: The Manager's Complete Guide to Teams in Organizations* (New Jersey: Prentice Hall, 1995).

Janis, I. L., *Groupthink: Psychological Studies of Policy Decisions and Fiascoes* (London: Houghton Mifflin, 1982).

Chapter Five

The Office Grapevine: Gossip, Politics and Power at Work

The Aim

Career advancement – powering your way to promotion through wise use of office politics.

Power-games.

Networking.

The office grapevine.

All unofficial, unregulated and partially uncontrollable aspects of the organisation; but they remain extremely effective for gaining information. And gaining information is absolutely vital for getting ahead.

However, although they provide access to information, power, politics, sex and gossip are all minefields. Picking your way successfully through them will not only leave you unscathed but also teach you how to profit from these potentially explosive areas.

Power does not reside only with your superiors, but in many different places. Empowering yourself by seizing some of this hidden power is the first step to success in this area of office life.

Acknowledging the role of power in the workplace leads to recognising the role of politics generally in the office – love it, or hate it, you can't ignore it, but you can benefit from it.

Within the tangle of organisational politics lies sexual politics. Unless you work in a monastery or a nunnery, your inevitable encounter with office sexual politics needs to be handled with care.

Hot on the heels of office relationships, of course, comes gossip. How does information spread and the political structure develop? The power of the office grapevine in gathering important and less important information should never be underestimated.

Sometimes, the gossip might be aimed at you. Perhaps the rumours are true; perhaps not. Either way, being gossiped about is unpleasant – but not disastrous; countering it takes you one step further towards making the grapevine work for you.

1. Power, Politics, Gossip... Can't I Just Ignore Them?

No.

Admittedly, most people have a very negative view of gossip, politics and power-games. Such concepts are seen as unnecessary and unwanted parts of the work environment, getting in the way of 'real' work. Some teleworkers believe that one of the greatest advantages of working from home lies in escaping the politicking and backstabbing that constitute such a large area of organisational life.

Certainly, at one time, a worker could ignore the gossip, refuse to play power-games, sidle away from the grapevine and not even know what a 'network' was.

Not any more. Today's worker is continually competing for jobs, promotion and recognition. Getting your head down and working will not necessarily be sufficient to gain you promotion: these days, politicking, networking and power-seeking are essential features of the modern office.

Are They Immoral?
No.

Power-seeking is not... feeding your ego.
Power-seeking is... increasing your ability to obtain resources fairly.

Politicking is not... gaining an unfair advantage.
Politicking is... increasing your access to power and influence.

Networking is not... using people for your own ends.
Networking is... constructing a web of contacts for the benefit of all concerned.

2. The Power Games Minefield

In organisations, those who have power are the first to know what's going on; the first to be consulted about things. Their opinions are valued. They frequently have access to materials that may be scarce or in great demand. Is it any wonder that so many of us yearn for power?

Do You Have Power?
Ask yourself these questions:

- do you find it difficult to work the expected long hours or weekends, due to family or other commitments?

- do you find that meetings are sometimes scheduled at times that are difficult for you to attend: for example, at breakfast?

- do you often feel that people at work talk about matters that you know little about: for example, case studies with which you are not involved, or even sport?

- do things get decided in meetings to which you are not invited?

- do some people at work belong to the same health club, drink together or play sport together?

- do people hold 'informal' meetings without you: for example, in the toilets, café or corridors?

Results
If you have answered 'yes' to more than three of these questions, it is time to seize some power!

The sources of power lie not just with the boss but in many different places...

Source of Power: Formal Authority
'Formal Authority' is the official power that we associate with the boss; or with those who have worked their way up the organisation. The fact that they have earned their right to this authority means that we tend to respect such people.

The power of these individuals rests in their control over that which we value most – our jobs. They have the power to hire or fire; to reward or punish; to make our lives heaven... or hell.

How to gain power here: build relationships with your superiors
This involves getting on with them, showing them respect and earning their respect.

> **Golden Rule**
> Do whatever is necessary to make you stand out from the others. When superiors make decisions that may affect your future, you will appear in a positive light.

Source of Power: Resource Control
Every organisation has its scarce resources. For some companies this can be money, for others the scarce resources are materials or stationery. In these situations, it is the person who holds the purse-strings, the key to the stationery cupboard, or the lunch vouchers, who wields power.

> In one company, ballpoint pens were always going missing. Supplies were so scarce that they were carefully controlled by an administrator, who distributed them in return for favours – gaining information, perhaps, or gossip. Access to this information allowed her to advance her career within the workplace; and that is how she used power.

How to gain power here: build relationships with those who control resources
Andrew, a computer salesman, was trying to gain access to a 'scarce resource' – the buyer in a large multinational company. The 'gatekeeper' of these scarce resources was the buyer's PA, who constantly refused to put him through to the buyer. Andrew takes up the story:

"Every time I called, the buyer was 'in a meeting'. Instead of getting angry with the PA, I tried to befriend her. I was very pleasant to her when I called, cracked jokes and asked how she was. I engaged her in conversation and worked hard at cultivating a positive relationship. This set me apart straight away from the other

salespeople who usually took out their anger on her – as I would have done in the past. Eventually, she started to sympathise with me and she must have told her boss to speak to me because I eventually gained access."

Few people realise that it is essential to cultivate good working relationships with those who control scarce resources. Like Andrew, you should no longer see these people as enemies, but as friends; and they will come to feel similarly about you.

Source of Power: Information Control

Even more powerful is the person who controls the information flow within the organisation and who possesses knowledge that is often withheld from others.

This person knows what happened in a secret meeting; knows the procedures for accessing funding; and knows the name of every client on the books. Such people are often in secretarial or personal assistant roles.

How to gain power here: gain information

Go on courses; read; learn. Become the only office expert in a certain area. Study another language that no one else in the office speaks – next time a German client calls, you will be the one in demand.

> **Golden Rule**
> Remember: anyone who knows something that someone else doesn't is in a position of power.

Source of Power: Technological Control

Today's organisations are usually dependent on some form of core technology as a means of survival and success; the worker who is able to use such technology is the one with the power.

Most people can use basic word-processing packages, but workers who know how to fix printer jams; troubleshoot when things go wrong; obtain any piece of information from the internet; or even mend photocopiers, are those who have the edge over their colleagues.

How to gain power here: become a technology expert

Learn how to troubleshoot with technology and you will be in demand when things go wrong. Your willingness – or not – to share these skills will give you power.

> Familiarise yourself with the workings of the computer, printer, fax, overhead projector and the all-important photocopier.
>
> Learn about newer technology, such as how to produce slides direct from a laptop PC.
>
> Learn valuable internet skills, such as building a web page – an ability you could use for the company and to promote your career.

Source of Power: Informal Networks

Networking is used by workers to fill the gaps in formal or official corporate communications; to do one another potentially returnable favours; to enhance organisational morale; and to advance careers.

How to gain power here: build a network

Building up a good network of contacts is crucial for gaining power. Networking is all about meeting people and about finding a path 'in' so that you can call up later requesting information, advice, or even a favour.

See everyone as a potential addition to your network. Exchange cards, then drop your

Some practitioners of networking estimate that over half of all management jobs come through personal contact, not through advertisements.

contacts a line occasionally to let them know you are still there. As your collection of cards grows, you will be increasingly able to call upon favours from many people in many companies, again, enhancing your access to power.

> **Golden Rule**
> Don't think that you are 'using' people: anybody with any sense will be doing the same to you.

Source of Power: Symbols

Physical settings, appearances and styles of behaviour can add immensely to a person's power if they are perceived to represent authority.

SEE CHAPTER 1

How to gain power here: dress for success

Dress to impress – understand you company's dress code, and dress towards the upper end of this.

[Source: Morgan, 1986; Mann, 1995]

3. The Political Minefield

"I avoid all the political games at work. I haven't got the time or energy to get involved with all that rubbish."

David, Financial Consultant

"I hate all the politicking that goes with the job. My job would be great if it weren't for the political games."

Sarah, Client Services Manager

"Politics? I come to work to do a job and I do it to the best of my ability. I am relying on my work performance to get ahead, not on my politicking skills. Otherwise I would have gone into politics!"

Ed, Salesperson

Organisational politics: destructive, bitchy and manipulative or necessary work skills for the twenty-first century office?

The indisputable reality is that politics are an important aspect of organisational life, and no amount of head-buried-in-the-sand behaviour (see examples above) can change this fact.

You have to know how to politick.

Why Politick?
Politicking will...

...ensure that people generally know you.

...ensure that important people are aware of what you are doing.

...enable you to call in favours when you need them.

...give you access to 'hidden' information.

...give you access to power and to influence.

Aristotle, the Ancient Greek philosopher, advocated politics as a less autocratic way of tackling the diverse interests of the *polis*, or state inhabitants. Thus 'politics' are not intended to cause friction between groups of people with different interests, but instead to recognise and reconcile competing interests.

Organisations are political, then, because their members are diverse, and only a 'political' system can, as Aristotle established, recognise the varied interests of these members.

How to Politick

Step 1: Understand your organisation
Understand the processes, procedures and systems of your working environment. Work out the informal systems that control the organisation, and establish the power bases. Make sure that you know what the (official and unofficial) hierarchy is.

Step 2: Get involved
Involve yourself in as many of the 'backroom' systems as you can. Join committees, working groups, boards, management groups – in fact, anything that will help get you known, and that will help you uncover more about the ways in which the organisation operates.

Golden Rule
Remember: the point of joining a committee is not only to attain the goal of the group in question but also to gain access to power and powerful people.

Step 3: Meet people in your company
Once you have identified certain people as a source of power, attempt to meet them. Introduce yourself: state who you are and what you do.

Step 4: Meet people in other companies
Attend training days and workshops or conferences to expand your knowledge base, and your list of contacts.

Be pleasant and engaging; offer to do favours; look up a piece of information; send one of your contacts a useful address; or a relevant article you have read. You will then be in a position to ask for a repayment of that favour, should you ever need it – if, for example, you are looking for a new post.

Step 5: Be visible
Keep everybody regularly updated about your progress and achievements.

Example:
Dear Pete,
Hi, how are you? I just thought you might be interested to hear that my meeting with AB Co. went very well, and I have secured the contract.
Yours,
Jane

Example:
Dear Helen,
We haven't spoken for a while; I thought you might be pleased to know that the entry I prepared for the best in-house magazine competition came third.
Yours,
Robert

Step 6: Find a mentor
Try to find an individual within the organisation who is more experienced and knowledgeable than you. Arrange to meet them perhaps once a month, on an informal basis, in order to chat. Your advisor will be able to introduce you to a lot of people they know and you may also benefit from any favours they can call in.

Step 7: Socialise
Socialise regularly with work colleagues. If there is an established ritual such as going to a certain pub, join in.

Golden Rule
Remember: some of the most important business is conducted after hours.

Note

While this chapter is devoted particularly to the workings of politics and power within the workplace, the subject of politics recurs frequently in many different areas of this book as a whole, as a system that will enable you to negotiate your way through the workplace.

Impression Management in particular is very important for introducing the reader to the politics of appearance and behaviour, and directly complements this chapter on politics, information and power.

SEE CHAPTER 1

4. The Sexual Minefield

It is almost impossible to escape one of the most visible and fraught areas of office politics: sexual politics.

When we look for romantic partners, we look – consciously or otherwise – for things in common; shared interests. What stronger shared interest could there be than something we spend most of our time doing: work? We also spend more time at work than we do anywhere else; it is hardly surprising, then, that relationships develop in the office.

The Situations

There are three different kinds of sexual relationship situations in the office.

Situation 1: Both partners are free to become involved with each other (neither is married or has a partner) and both are willing.

Situation 2: One partner is not free or both partners are not free.

Situation 3: One partner is unwilling to engage in the proposed relationship.

Each situation is fraught with hazards, both for those involved and for onlookers, and must be navigated with care.

Situation 1: Both Partners are Free; Both are Willing

Why are office relationships so unpopular?

Onlookers invariably find the coy smiles and canoodling of a couple excruciatingly annoying in office situations. Office romances can interrupt the concentration of both partners, and a romantic relationship often disrupts the objectivity and rationality that should exist in the office: one partner may well try to do favours for the other in a manner not beneficial to team goals.

If the relationship ends, it may well become very unpleasant or impossible for both parties to continue working with each other.

Guidelines for this situation

- Don't hold hands or touch each other at work or even as you come into work.

- Don't go for lunch with your partner every day.

- Don't let your feelings cloud your judgement.

- Don't engage in secret jokes or talk.

How to deal with the office couple

"It started as a bit of a laugh. I work in a team of three and the other two started a romance. But after a bit it became less funny – you know, something for me to rib the bloke about in the gents – and more of a serious threat to our team output. The two of them were forever late and would waltz in, giggling like schoolkids. Worse, they would often come in the next morning, having discussed or decided some issue in their pillow talk the night before! They would always agree with each other and if I disagreed, they ganged up on me. It became a nightmare, as I was convinced that they were not making rational decisions or producing quality work.

"Eventually, they split up... and then it was even worse! They would not talk to each other and they kept passing messages through me. They would bicker and argue. They could not agree on anything.

"I only solved the problem by getting a new job. But I feel sorry for whoever took my place."

Patrick, Account Executive

In such a situation, it is best to approach the members of the couple separately, and explain the problem. Do not tackle the couple together – that allows them the psychological advantage of support from each other. People are more likely to be reasonable on their own.

Golden Rule
If one partner is in a superior position, the relationship really should be kept quiet. Rightly or wrongly, no one will believe that the boss can treat two workers fairly if one of them is the boss's sexual partner.

Situation 2: Both Partners are Willing, but not Free

"If I knew someone was having an affair, I would lose all respect for them. In fact, I would not trust them or want to do business with them. If they cannot be trusted by their partner, how can I trust them?"

Joel, Managing Director

Inevitably, if you are involved in such a relationship you will be judged – and usually unfavourably. People will lose faith and trust in you: this is why politicians and public figures have been forced to resign over affairs of the heart.

Guidelines for this situation
- Make a point of keeping quiet about your relationship.

- Don't consider it safe to show affection anywhere in public – eventually someone will spot you.

- Try to avoid appearing to be in love. People in the throes of a new passion often smile more, whistle, sing and walk with a spring in their step. Previously grumpy workers positively beam when asked to make the coffee... such is the power of love.

- Similarly, avoid dressing in an obviously different manner or dramatically changing your appearance.

- Try not to over-compensate by pointedly ignoring each other, especially if you used to communicate regularly.

- Don't look guilty in what could be innocent situations: for example, springing apart if 'caught' talking.

Note

The advice in this book is intended only to help you succeed and advance at work; no moral standpoint will be taken on the subject of affairs. In terms of your career, however, you should be aware that a relationship of this nature at work will almost certainly not help your prospects.

Despite this, such relationships may develop at work and it is a situation that must be handled with great care. You should probably expect things to be difficult; and expect also that people will view you with disapproval.

I'm Not the One Having an Affair...

If it is not you indulging in an illicit affair but one of your colleagues, then you may find yourself in an awkward position. If you personally know the cheated partner, you are, by association, colluding with the cheater.

Should you tell? Are you expected to cover for your colleague?

Guidelines for this situation

- If asked, be wary about lying for your colleague.

- Remember, though, that it is not your place to inform the cheated partner of the deceit.

- If asked difficult questions by the cheated partner, use your discretion; perhaps respond with polite but vague answers, along the lines of:

  "I don't know where they are."
  Or:
  "I'll see they get the message."

- If asked directly by the cheated party if their partner is having an affair, respond by saying:

  "You really should ask x [name of partner] *themselves."*

My Boss is Having an Affair

What if it is your boss asking you to cover for them?

This situation is significantly more difficult since your boss is obviously in a position either to reward or to punish you. If you refuse to co-operate, there is always the worry that your boss could make life difficult for you.

Guidelines for this Situation

Do the minimum amount necessary in order to keep things running smoothly with your boss – but make it clear to them how uncomfortable it makes you feel.

If you are strong and brave enough to say 'No', tell them why; add that you hope your working relationship will not be adversely affected. Remind your boss that you are normally co-operative and always willing to do any work-related task required.

Golden Rule

Be wary about agreeing to cover for someone else's affair.

Situation 3: One Person is Not Willing

This highly contentious and extremely dangerous area of sexual politics is also known as harassment. Harassment occurs when one individual steps over the boundaries of what is acceptable behaviour for both sexes in the workplace.

What are the boundaries?

Behavioural boundaries in the office are often dictated by the attitude with which the behaviour is accompanied.

Remarks which in many situations would be seen as innocent can take on a potentially offensive and sexist air if accompanied by the wrong attitude. For example, a person known for his egalitarian attitude to men and women is less likely to cause offence by inadvertently assuming a particular boss being referred to is male. A person with a known sexist attitude is likely to cause irritation and offence if he makes the same assumption. Similarly, a man who has a respectful attitude towards women in terms of seeing them as equal workers is less likely to be accused of deliberate harassment if he accidentally touches a woman in the office than a man who is known to leer at women.

Differences of opinion, background and age can also lead to conflicting sexual politics in the office. For example, older male workers may be used to calling women 'darling' or 'love', which many women today find offensive. Women too can be instigators of offence; more and more cases of sexual harassment by women are being brought to the courts.

If you're being harassed

If you find yourself subject to unwelcome advances, remember: it is not your fault. Many people fail to take action against the source of harassment, feeling that they are somehow responsible. Assuming that you have made your feelings clear, then it is never your fault.

Keep a diary or record of any unwelcome advances made. Try to get witnesses; find out if anyone else is being subjected to these attentions.

Take action. Report the offender to superiors or, if necessary, seek advice from your union representative.

Sexual Politics: How to Avoid Being Misinterpreted

Think about what you're saying

Don't say anything to a woman that you couldn't say to a man – and vice versa.

Example:

If, as a man, you feel it is friendly to admire your female colleagues' clothes, consider whether you would say 'nice trousers' to your male colleague.

Treat everybody as individuals

You should ignore gender differences and treat men and women as individuals. At work you can put aside your prejudices – you are dealing with people, not men and women.

Treat touching with caution

Being 'touchy-feely' is fine if you confine touches to the forearm area. In some environments it is acceptable to touch the upper arm. Always be wary about touching someone anywhere other than the areas mentioned above.

Know the etiquette

Whoever goes through a door first should open it for the person behind: a simple rule which avoids any gender issues.

Don't generalise

Avoid such stereotyping comments as the following:

"All men are incapable of feeling emotion."

"Of course you can't fix the photocopier: you're a woman."

Don't get physical

Avoid commenting on anyone's anatomy or body, whether they be work colleagues, customers, or even passers-by.

Don't assume

Don't take it for granted that everyone in the office is heterosexual. Chances are that one in ten will be gay/lesbian. To avoid causing offence, politely enquire after 'partners' rather than 'boyfriends' or 'girlfriends'.

Don't assume, either, that married women will take on their husband's name, or want to be called 'Mrs'.

Women can be as guilty of 'sexist' comments as men. One woman who often admired the way that certain men 'filled' their shirts, was oblivious to the fact that this was offensive.

Avoid gender specific language

Do not automatically refer to managers as 'he' or secretaries as 'she', particularly in written communication – it is very likely that you will cause offence.

Instead, use 'he or she'; or simply, 'they'.

Don't tolerate sexism

Don't laugh at sexist or homophobic jokes. If you are genuinely offended, or think that somebody else might be, the most non-confrontational method of dealing with this is simply to turn away or change the subject. This subtly registers your distaste without making a big deal about it. If you are able, it might be possible to say, "Actually, I'm sure some people would find that a bit offensive. Has anyone ever mentioned that before?" Such a comment would bring the subject into the open, while avoiding a heavy-handed approach.

You should generally refuse to endorse any other kind of sexist behaviour, from either men or women.

Finally...

Whether you're a man or a woman, *never* accuse a woman of being 'pre-menstrual'.

> **Golden Rule**
> The key to avoiding problems is to treat all workers in a respectful and courteous manner, as individuals with rights.

5. The Gossiping Minefield

"The managers look down on gossip – they're always saying, 'Oh, have you been gossiping again?' when we ask them to confirm a rumour we have heard. Yet the grapevine is often the only way we get information – the managers would never tell us off their own bat."

Alice, Human Resources Assistant

"We never hear anything of importance through any official sources. Threats of redundancies, mergers, new car-parking arrangements... whatever it is, we always find out on the grapevine. I'm sure someone somewhere must be responsible for 'leaking' information into the system so that we have to scramble for pieces of information rather than have it presented to us properly."

Sharif, Accounts Assistant

"The staff are always gossiping! There is always some rumour or other flying around. They have nothing better to do than tittle-tattle. It's no wonder we don't bother having briefings... these things get round much quicker on the grapevine."

Chloë, Field Marketing Manager

Gossip. Valuable and necessary for employees; negative and annoying for managers; essential for you to understand if you want to progress in the workplace.

The Advantages of Gossip

Obtaining information
"Rumours had been flying about a possible merger of our company with another. Along with that were rumours about mass redundancies. Some people dismissed it as mere gossip, especially when the managers denied it all. But I took it very seriously, and I started looking for a new job. I figured that if I found a better job, I'd go even if the rumours were false. In the end, redundancies were announced a month later but I had the advantage of already having interviews lined up."

Conrad, Computer Engineer

Possibly the best benefit of gossip is its ability to obtain important information. The information most frequently communicated through the gossip grapevine tends to be about redundancy threats, promotional prospects or new job openings; hence, as Conrad discovered, you will be able to take action quickly.

Obtaining inside information
"I was listening to my colleagues gossiping about my boss's interest in line dancing. They were all having a good laugh, but I stored the information and at Christmas I bought her a line dancing tape. She was thrilled and always had a soft spot for me after that... which did me no harm!"

Fiona, Customer Service Representative

Gossip can enable you to obtain inside information that will help you to progress within your current job.

Bonding with colleagues
The experience of sharing exclusive information can enable the forging of a bond; the bond is enhanced if the information is a 'secret' between the two of you.

Although they denigrate it, managers may rely on gossip to avoid confronting staff about changes or new regulations and on occasions find it equally as useful as employees do.

Gossip also offers colleagues the opportunity to develop a shared interest and engage in in-depth conversation, while discussing the rumour and planning its possible consequences.

The Disadvantages of Gossip

Inaccuracy of information
Rupert heard a rumour that he and a few colleagues were being moved to a different branch in another part of the city. He acted on the information by spending time building up a case against the move, with breakdowns of the transport costs and a petition from colleagues. It turned out that the rumour was untrue and his boss was rather annoyed about the time Rupert had wasted on his little project.

Before you pay too much attention to the rumour in question, remember that gossip may be exaggerated and inaccurate; and it might not be wise to act too quickly on the information received.

The possibility of bias

"I was warned on my first day to be wary of Sheila as she was rumoured to be two-faced. I heeded the advice and was quite cool towards her, turning down her offers of help and advice. After two years, we have become very good friends – she is brilliant and not two-faced at all. I really missed out on the help she could have given me in those early days."

Philippa, Graphic Designer

There is a possibility that gossip can unfairly bias your views about another person, bringing prejudice to bear on your first impression of them.

Gossip may backfire

Sometimes if you pass on gossip it could backfire, and you may be accused of being a gossipmonger. Alternatively, if you don't pass on the gossip, you run the risk of being perceived as aloof.

Profiting from Office Gossip

Listen to it. Don't refuse to hear, or you might be viewed negatively by your colleagues. You might also miss out on some important information.

Don't be tempted to add snippets of your own – the phenomenon of 'psychological reciprocity' means that the urge to respond with your own revelations is strong. [Source: Settoon, Bennett, Liden, 1996] Resist it. Make neutral remarks like "Uh-huh"; "Is that right"; and such-like. This is what counsellors do to remain neutral but interested.

Contrary to what is commonly known about the accuracy (or otherwise) of gossip, one study actually estimated that three quarters of grapevine information is, in fact, accurate. [Source: Walton, 1961]

Once you have received the information, try to change the subject. Thus you will avoid being seen as a gossip yourself, but won't be seen as aloof.

Try to keep an open mind about what you are told; don't let it unduly cloud your judgement, or influence your opinions. At the same time, don't completely discard the information: store it in the back of your mind – you never know when it might be useful. Most importantly, be cautious about passing on gossip in order not to be perceived in a negative light.

If a person is continually gossiping, they may be doing so because of a need to raise their own self-esteem. It is, after all, powerful to hold information about another individual. Try to meet those needs in other ways by asking the person for advice or complimenting them on their work.

Research has shown that people who say negative things about others are often perceived to possess the negative traits about which they are gossiping. This is a transference effect: the traits you are gossiping about in others about are transferred to you. [Source: Jung, 1974]

Our memories recall things through association; we associate the gossiper with the gossip. The interaction with the gossiper will remain more firmly in the mind of the listener than the information actually passed on.

In other words, if x tells y that z is manipulative, y will instead remember x (not z) as manipulative.

6. I Trod on a Mine – the Gossip's About Me

"I became aware of a rumour flying round the office that I was having an affair with the boss. The boss lived near me and would often give me a lift to work, but he was happily married and there was absolutely nothing untoward going on. I didn't know what to do, and it was a bit embarrassing to tell my boss. No one asked me directly if anything was going on, so how could I deny it?"

Rebecca, Assistant Brand Manager

The gossip about you may stem from jealousy, boredom or fun; it may be justified; it may not. It is a situation in which many – unsuspecting – individuals have found themselves, and it is one that requires a careful strategy to beat the gossip.

Rebecca continues: *"In the end, I confronted a couple of colleagues and asked them exactly what was being said about me. It was incredible – according to the gossip, the boss was about to leave his wife and kids for me! I realised that someone must have been starting the rumours, so I asked everyone where they heard it from. I never actually found the original source – people seem to protect each other and close ranks. But by asking I was demonstrating that I would not put up with the malicious gossip. I told everyone how irritating the rumours were. I hinted too that it was unfounded slander. Then I found some excuse to bring my real boyfriend into the office so they could see how happy we were. I put up his photo on my desk too. My colleagues soon got the message and the gossiping stopped."*

Step 1: Identify the rumour
Ask friendly colleagues to tell you what is being said; some gentle persuasion may be necessary. Tell them how unhappy the rumour is making you and how helpful it would be to know exactly what it was.

Step 2: Identify the source of the rumour
Ask colleagues to tell you who told them. Explain that you are not blaming anyone, but that it would help to know where the rumour originated. It could be that the source overheard something, or misunderstood something you said or did. By discovering the originator of the rumour, you can attempt to put them right.

Step 3: Discredit or counter the rumour

Dominic discovered a rumour saying that he was leaving the company. It was true, he was, but he didn't want his bosses to know just yet. He started another rumour – he was being promoted.

Suppose what is being spread about you is actually true? How do you discredit the truth? You could do as Dominic did – spread a rumour that contradicts the truth of the existing one.

If the rumour is a complete fabrication, you could again use the 'counter-rumour' technique above. Alternatively, confront the source of the gossip and ask them to pass around some more gossip – that the first rumour was simply not true.

Step 4: In extreme cases, take further action

If the rumours are libellous, destroying your character and reputation, or could negatively affect your career prospects, consider speaking directly to your superiors to explain the situation. It might help if you can take with you evidence to help prove that the rumour simply isn't true.

If this doesn't quash the rumour, you could consider taking legal action; but be careful about threatening such action if you do not intend actually to take it. If you are a member of a trade union, consult your steward before doing anything else.

Chapter Checkpoint

After reading this chapter, you should:

- know about power games and sources of power in the workplace.

- have insight into the workings of office politics.

- understand the perils and pitfalls of office romances and sexual politics.

- know the advantages and disadvantages of office gossip.

- be able to respond if you are the victim of the office grapevine.

In the Next Chapter

How to communicate effectively using the new and old media of the office.

Further Reading

Tannen, D., *Talking from 9 to 5: Men and Women at Work* (London: Virago, 1996).

Pfeffer, J., *Managing with Power: Politics and Influence in Organizations* (Cambridge, Mass: Harvard Business School Press, 1992).

Baird, R. B., *The Executive Grapevine* (London: Executive Grapevine Publications, 1983).

Chapter Six

Getting the Message: Communication at Work

The Aim

Career advancement – maximising your communication skills; maximising your promotion prospects.

David is a quality control manager for a large company. His day starts at 8.30 a.m. when he arrives at his desk. The first thing he does is check his voice mail for any messages that may have been left since yesterday afternoon when he was last in his office.

There are five voice mails and three answerphone messages (David's voice mail picks up when his phone is engaged). Of those, four need calling back, which he does immediately. Of the four he calls back, he only gets through to one – he leaves messages for the other three, either with secretaries or on answerphones.

The other four messages require different responses: to one person he faxes a copy of a report with a covering note; another message he passes on to his own manager, putting it in her pigeon-hole with a memo.

The remaining two he decides to respond to by email.

It's now 9.15 a.m., and David switches on his computer and logs on. He has 23 emails, and he works quickly through the list. Some can be responded to by email, some require phone calls, others letters and faxes. Three messages cannot yet be responded to properly, as he needs to gather the required information; he thus sends each of them a quick email to tell them this. Eventually, he sends emails in response to the three phone messages he had.

The time is now 10.45 a.m., but David is not yet finished at his computer. He needs to inform both his manager and his subordinates of some information that he has received from his emails. He thinks for a moment, then decides to send one email to his staff on their user-group (one message can be sent to all of them at once), and also sends it separately to his boss, with an extra note requesting a meeting to discuss the contents. He gets an immediate response from his boss who arranges a meeting for 12 noon.

David notices that he now has five new email messages which came in while he was writing, but he can't respond to them just yet because his phone is ringing. He answers the phone, deals with a query from one of his subordinates, and puts the phone down. Immediately his voice mail rings to say that he has another message; he rings in to the system, only to find a query from another subordinate about the same matter.

David thinks for a moment, then decides to call a brief meeting to answer the queries face-to-face. He moves back to his computer and sends another email to all his staff, asking that they be available at 11.45 a.m. for a quick brief on a matter that has already caused a few queries.

It is already 11.20 a.m., and David quickly finishes his email correspondence. The next task is the regular mail. He has eight letters, all of which need responding to, either with letters of reply, phone calls, faxes or emails. He doesn't have time for all of them so, with a sigh, puts them on his in-tray.   David rushes off to meet his staff at 11.45 a.m. then straight to meet his boss at 12 noon.

Another typical morning.

Whatever field you are in, you will probably spend a great deal of your time in communication activities.

Until recently, communication was limited to phone calls, letters or face-to-face meetings. Now the choice of communication media is bewildering. Communication is not just part of your job: it is something that needs to be handled carefully and skilfully to get your message across, and make yourself clear to colleagues.

Since communication is so important, you should know how to effectively use the range of media available to you. Your telephone skills, for example, may appear to be good, but there is always room for improvement and for refining your ability to communicate well by telephone. Phones are also increasingly dependent on messaging systems: how can answerphones and voice mails be used effectively?

Many people now use email, of course – and this new and incredibly widespread form of media has its own rules, all of which need to be understood and followed. For example, how do you know when to use email and when to make a phone call? Or when to send a memo instead of calling a meeting? And how to write it? Or how to correctly address a letter, for that matter?

And communication doesn't start or end with written messages: you'll also be using it in meetings and presentations. Nor does communication consist solely of words – body language speaks volumes, and can either enhance or contradict what you say verbally.

Your guide to successful and effective communication starts here.

1. Communicating – the Principle

Why It Matters

"I was contacted by a subordinate of mine who was teleworking. She emailed me to say she was sending a report over. 'Great,' I thought. She then sent it as an attached file by email, which I printed out. It was 12 pages long, and not terribly urgent, so I was a bit peeved that she sent it this way – I felt the post would have been better. Still, I mentally congratulated her on her keenness. Two hours later, a 12-page fax of the same document appeared in my pigeon-hole. I was surprised she had sent it twice, but thought she was just being careful. The faxed copy was a little clearer than the emailed one, so I tore off each of the 12 pages and stapled them together. The next morning, I received in the post yet another copy of the document! I was more than a little annoyed – if I had known she was going to send me a mailed copy, I

would not have wasted time tearing the faxed one or printing out the emailed copy; to say nothing of all that wasted paper. And, to cap it all, she rang me to check I had received her document!"

Mahmood, Sales Manager

"I am a manager of eight staff and I recently sent them all an email requesting that they attend a particular meeting. To me it was a simple request with no hidden meaning. But boy did this erupt! They read all sorts of things into it, like I was making a big deal about them missing meetings, or that I was ordering them about. You see, I am a very laissez-faire type boss and meetings are normally voluntarily attended. Not many people had been attending, so I sent this email. But I wasn't telling them off – simply asking that they make the effort with this one. They perceived it as being told off, as a change in managerial style, as a change of policy... in retrospect, I wish I had not used email to send my message as they were not able to see from my face that I was not telling them off."

Tara, Production Manager

"Our boss called a meeting once to give us some instructions on new assembly techniques. The meeting was at quite an inconvenient time for many of us and three teleworkers came in especially for it. The instructions were very straightforward and we felt irritated that he had called us for a meeting. Why could he not have emailed them to us, or sent them as photocopies? Then we could have looked at them in our own time and not wasted time going to a pointless meeting!"

Denzil, Computer Engineer

In their barest form, communication skills are one of the most basic elements of human ability, but many workers – as the examples show – do not know how to use them properly, or even what they really are.

In its most refined form, communication involves:

- making yourself clearly understood verbally.
- communicating with clarity in the written medium.
- being able to select the right medium to communicate your message.
- knowing when you do not understand others, or when they have problems understanding you.

Many employees are good in at least one of these areas, but few are proficient in all of them. A good communicator has the advantage of being able to get their message across and they will thus have greater influence in the workplace. A good communicator will also impress others; and a good impression is always vital.

What It Is

Communication is the transfer of information from sender to receiver.

Such is the common definition of communication. This particular definition, although common, is incomplete and frequently leads to poor communication.

What such an interpretation fails to do is to take account of the most important element of communication: the receiver.

The Receiver

Communication is when the sender creates a message that is understood by the receiver.

Such is the complete definition of communication. It should never occur in a vacuum. Whatever the medium is, always consider the other party very carefully.

The aim should not be simply to send a message to the recipient but rather to develop a shared meaning with them. This makes the receiver of the message part of the process, and means that communication is not achieved unless the message has been not only received but also understood.

> **According to one study, there are more than 100 definitions of communication.** [Source: Dance and Larson, 1976]

2. Communicating – by Telephone

The telephone is the most interactive of all the communication media. Remember also that telephone communication is time-specific: in other words, the receiver is likely to be interrupted and must take the message immediately (unless they are using answerphones or voice mail).

The telephone also requires an instant response, and is thus the most interactive of all the communication media.

The Phone – the Right Medium When...
- You need an immediate response from or a discussion with the other person.

- You don't need to record that the communication took place or produce any evidence of what was said at a later stage.

- You are not worried about things getting heated or one of you getting angry – people can say things on the phone that they may regret.

Making the Call
Many people find using the phone difficult – particularly when they cannot see the other person's face – and would thus benefit from a clear guide towards what to say and how to say it. However, even the most confident phone user will find the following section useful.

Step 1: Can I speak to...
Ask for the person you want clearly, using their correct name and title.

Step 2: My name is...
State your full name, even if the other person knows who you are – it is very common to receive a phone call from Emma or John, and then to spend the next ten minutes trying to work out which Emma or John it is.

Also tell the recipient which company you are calling from; even if you are working from home.

> People rarely modify their 'script' when the person they want answers the phone themselves. Resist the temptation to start a conversation like this:
> *"Elizabeth Thomson speaking."*
> *"Oh, hello, is that Elizabeth Thomson?"*

Step 3: I'm calling because...
Always have a clear purpose in your mind. Stating your purpose should provide the receiver with an indication of how long the call might take; they can then decide if they have the time to talk. If the call is being made just to 'touch base' then this is a valid purpose that should be expressed.

Step 4: Is it convenient...?
You might at this point want to check that the recipient has the time to deal with your query at that moment or whether they would prefer to speak at a later time. A polite, "Is it convenient to speak about this now?" should do the trick.

Step 5: Let me explain...
You can now embark on a more detailed discussion of your subject.

Step 6: Goodbye...
Thank the person for their time. Indicate what you will do next or what you would like them to do next. This is always a positive way to end a call.

Example:
"Right, thanks for your time. I'll get that article to you by next Monday and meanwhile, I'll watch out for the contract in the post."

Receiving a Call
Some of the advice below is appropriate only for those who have a direct line; some of it is designed for shared-line users.

Step 1: Hello...
When answering, make sure you introduce yourself by announcing both your first name and surname. Apart from confirming who you are to the caller, this gives the impression of professionalism and control. In addition, asking how you can help always conveys a very positive impression.

Example:
"Hello, [your name], *how may I help you?"*
Try to keep a smile in your voice, and avoid carrying over any baggage from

a previous conversation. You may have just been told off by your boss, but you should still answer the phone with a bright and positive greeting.

Step 2: It's not for you...
Always ask politely who is calling.

> **Example:**
> *"Who shall I say is calling?"*
> or
> *"May I ask who's calling?"*

Don't immediately admit that the person is there – just in case they can't take the call. Say, "I'll just see if they're free". Avoid saying, "I'll see if I can find them" – this makes it sound as if your colleague has gone AWOL.

If the other person can't take the call, you can then go back and say, "I'm afraid they have someone with them/are on another call/have just gone into a meeting." Be wary, however, of the 'meeting' excuse, as this is commonly perceived – rightly or wrongly – as meaning that the other person is avoiding the caller.

Ask if you can take a message, adding something along the lines of, "I'll get him/her to call you back as soon as possible." Never say, "They're at lunch"; "I don't know where they are"; or, "They're in the toilet." Saying that the other person is not at their desk is fine, but follow it up immediately with an offer to take a message.

Step 3: It is for you...
If it is not convenient to take the call or deal with the issue at that time, politely excuse yourself.

> **Example:**
> *"I'm sorry, I'm with somebody at the moment. Can I call you back shortly?"*

A General Guide to Using the Phone

Don't be nervous
It is difficult when you can't see the other person's facial expressions and body language, but being able to communicate well on the phone is a valuable asset. Try to avoid too many hesitations and don't be too long-winded.

Pause for breath
Because you cannot see the other person, turn-taking cues are missing. The other person's desire to speak is usually indicated visually by opening the mouth, taking a breath, moving forward, and so on; these are absent in phone conversations. The temptation, therefore, is to waffle on without a break. Don't. Take frequent pauses for breath, and if the other person hasn't interjected, invite them to with comments like, "What do you think?"; or, "Is there anything you'd like to ask?"

Take notes
It is very easy to misinterpret verbal communication, in the absence of written records of what was said. It is a good idea, therefore, to take notes during the conversation and to clarify points as you go along.

For an important conversation, it will make a good impression if you write to the recipient afterwards clarifying what was agreed. In general, you should do this only if you initiated the call.

Give your full attention

When speaking on the phone, you should give the other person your full attention. It may be acceptable to answer another line if it rings; but apologise first, or ask them if they mind. When you do answer the other line, simply tell the new caller that you are not available at present. Ideally, it is better to let the other call be picked up, if possible, by your answerphone or voice mail.

Again, with personal callers you should explain to the new visitor that you are taking a call and would they wait or come back later.

If you have a meeting scheduled, explain this to your caller at the start, unless the call has lasted an unusually long time, in which case it is acceptable simply to explain that you have to leave for a meeting.

Golden Rule

Never answer the phone whilst finishing a conversation with your colleague. This is terrible manners; and the caller hears something like:

"...and we ended up wrestling on the bed together. Jones and Jones, how can I help you?"

Answerphones and Voice Mail

Voice mail is a system built into the telephone itself. Your phone will usually ring you to tell you that there are new messages; you might then dial a special number to pick up your messages. With answerphones, of course, your messages are visibly indicated by a flashing red light and must be physically played back.

The advantage of voice mail over answerphones is that it can take messages even when you are on another call.

Personalised messages

Both answerphones and voice mail have the option of leaving a personalised recorded outgoing message to greet callers. Always opt for a personalised message. Your personalised message should include:

- your name; the name of your company; your phone number if appropriate.

- an indication of when you will be back at your desk and when you will return the call (if you're going to be away for longer than a day or more).

- the option of calling alternative numbers: include mobile numbers and so on.

- the option of using another medium to send the message: include your fax number or email address.

- a word of thanks for calling.

Golden Rule

Always smile when you record a message: this will help to keep your message upbeat and happy.

Leaving Messages

Step 1: Hello, it's...
Introduce yourself, saying which company you represent.

Step 2: I'm calling because...
State clearly and concisely the reason for your call. Don't go into lengthy or complex details at this point.

Step 3: Please give me a call
Indicate what further action you will take (for example, sending a fax); or what you would like them to do. Usually you will ask the person to call you back at their convenience; but you may prefer to call them back.

Step 4: My number is...
Leave your phone number, even if you have said you will call them back.

Golden Rule

Don't waffle, hesitate or say things like, "I hate talking on these machines..."

Mobile Phones

Taking calls

Receiving calls on a mobile phone should follow the same formula as answering a normal phone. If you are on a train or going through areas of interference, warn the caller that there may be some loss of reception. If you don't want to be interrupted, turn off your mobile phone. Callers should not be made to feel that they are an irritant for having called a mobile.

Making calls

Making calls to mobiles is no different to making calls on a normal phone, except that greater care should be taken to ensure that the recipient is able to speak. People often worry that because the other person is not at their desk they will catch them at an inconvenient moment. Remember, however, that the recipient has the option of switching off the phone if they are unable to talk.

Golden Rule

Be aware that it is dangerous – and illegal – to speak on the phone whilst driving. Always turn your phone off.

3. Communicating – by Email

What is Email?

Electronic mail, or 'email', uses the internet to transmit written messages between computer terminals instantaneously. Messages are typed on to the screen using a keyboard, and the communicator, who is 'logged on' to a network of computer users, can send a message to anyone else connected to this worldwide network.

Until the last decade, the majority of email users were universities, but now many companies are connected and many individuals have email at home as well. There is thus a very good chance that you can use your computer at work to send messages to friends in America and to your brother in Glasgow, as well as to your boss and to your colleagues. A connection to the internet will also allow you access to a wide range of information on the 'World Wide Web'.

Email – the Lingo

Email	Electronic mail.
Logging on	Connecting to the network.
Network	Connected system of computers.
Internet	A network of computers linked anywhere in the world through which information in many forms can be transmitted.
Intranet	An internet that is internal to a single organisation or site, and which allows you only to connect to other computers or information within the company.
World Wide Web	Worldwide computerised library or information system.
Usergroup	A group of computer users who share the same interest and are connected to a central provider.
Attached files	A means of sending a document to another computer user via email.
Modem	An electronic device to send information via phone connections.

When to Send an Email

Ensure that the receiver uses their email account

"I was looking to buy a house and noticed that the agent of the house I liked had an email address. I sent an email to express my interest in the property and waited. I expected an immediate response, but after two days I called to find out what was happening. They had never seen my email and made some excuse about having problems logging on. It was clear that they never used the email but just put their address on the letterhead to impress people. I lost the house."

Devi, Press and Publicity Assistant

Before you send an email, check that the receiver actually uses and reads their email. Many people have an email address simply to convey status or because their company automatically gives all its employees an address.

Ensure that the receiver checks their mail regularly

Some people only log on once a week, others three times a day. There is no point sending an urgent message to someone on Monday if they won't read it until Friday. The phone would be a better choice in this case.

Ensure that the message is simple

If the message is long, convoluted or complex, a phone call or standard letter may be better. Email is generally accompanied by an expectation of speed and simplicity, so receivers may be frustrated by long and convoluted messages.

Ensure that the subject of the message is informal

Email messages are, by their very nature, more informal than letters and may not be suitable for things such as formal agreements, contracts, disciplinary issues, and so on.

Golden Rule

Never use email if the contents are confidential or very private. There is no guarantee of confidentiality: always use letters for private information.

'Netiquette'

'Netiquette': another word for 'email etiquette'. As with any form of communication, email has its own guidelines about what you should or shouldn't do.

Finishing a message

Don't forget to 'sign off' at the end of your message. Many email systems allow you to add a 'signature' (your name, address and contact details) to the template which can be sent automatically with each message; but it is polite to sign off yourself as well.

Don't send 'flame mail'

'Flame mail' is another term for messages sent off in anger and often regretted later. You cannot fish an email out of a pile of post, so choose your words carefully.

Beware of chain messages

Be wary of passing on the numerous chain messages that often do the rounds. Passing on long emails to lots of other people will annoy those who don't wish to read this mail.

Golden Rule

Look at your email regularly: people will expect quick responses from you.

Be careful with your language

Emotions are not easily communicated in email. There are no facial expressions to accompany your message and, unlike during phone calls, you cannot rely upon tone of voice to convey what you feel. You may have to soften your language or tell the recipient directly about your emotion. Some people use 'smileys' in their emails: symbols which communicate the message-sender's feelings.

Smileys

:)	=	happy
: (	=	sad
: o	=	shocked
:&	=	confused

Note

'Smileys' are not considered appropriate for business use. Use them only when emailing friends or close colleagues; otherwise you risk being considered slightly immature or a time-waster.

Don't bombard people with emails

If you do have to send more than one email to a recipient within a short period of time indicate in the subject title the order in which the messages run.

Beware of 'joke material'

Be careful about sending jokes to work colleagues. The internet abounds with humour, some of it good, some of it sexist, and much of it very risqué. Think about the underlying message you are sending with the joke. Sending too many 'joke' emails will also suggest that you are not working very hard if you still have time to indulge in such non-work activities.

Be careful with personal emails

Guard against spending too much time on non-work emails. Some messages might be checked or read by the 'postmaster', and a lot of personal mail suggests that you are using work time (and resources) inappropriately.

Adopt good housekeeping systems for your messages: delete anything you don't need to keep and set up file managers for things that you do want to keep. Similarly, print out a hard copy of important emails and file this appropriately.

4. Communicating – by Letter, Fax or Memo

By Letter

When to use letters

Letters should be used for more formal messages or longer, more complicated ones. However, if your letter runs into pages and pages, call a meeting instead.

How to use letters more effectively

- Always obtain the recipient's correct name, title and spelling: people can get very annoyed if addressed incorrectly. Ring to confirm if you are not sure.

- Address people you haven't met as Mr, Ms or Dr, followed by their surname. If you have spoken to them at length, developed a rapport or emailed regularly, you may address them by their first name.

- Keep the letter as brief and to the point as possible. The recipient should know what you want by the end of the first paragraph.

- Close with 'Yours sincerely' if you have addressed the person by their title and surname. If you used their first name, you can use 'Regards', or even 'Kind Regards'.

- Sign off with your signature, below which should be your printed name, title and job title. If you have used the receiver's first name, it can be appropriate for your signature to contain only your first name, although your full name should always be printed below.

Some people do not like being automatically addressed as Mrs or Miss, as they do not want to be defined only by their marital status. Unless, therefore, you know that the recipient prefers to be called Mrs or Miss, always use Ms.

The common etiquette if you are writing a letter to an unknown recipient is 'Dear Sir', not 'Dear Sir/Madam'. However, this is understandably offensive to many women; the best thing is to try every available avenue to discover the name of the person you want to read your letter. The 'Sir/Madam' form of address should only ever be used as a very last resort.

By Fax

When to use faxes

Faxes should be used instead of email when the other person (or indeed, you) is not connected to the Net; when you wish to send documents or drawings which cannot be sent via a computer; or when you need to send an urgent copy of a letter which has also been mailed.

How to use faxes

Always include a covering letter on headed paper, containing the following information:

- your name and contact details.

- the other person's name and address.

- the words 'BY FAX' or 'FAX TRANSMISSION' and the date.

- an indication of how many pages are to follow.

- an indication of whether the material to be faxed is also being sent in the mail (hard copy), or by email.

By Memo

When to use memos

Memos should be used within the company and are interchangeable with email. A memo, however, gives the impression that the contents are not routine and thus can convey a better sense of urgency than an email. An email may be more effective in a company already inundated with memos.

How to use memos

- Always include your name and department, and the date.

- Include also the name of the recipient. If the memo is going to multiple recipients, list all the names, and tick the appropriate one on each copy.

- Keep it concise. Two-line memos are perfectly acceptable.

5. Communicating – in Meetings

Meetings are one of the most effective methods of communication, but many people resent them, saying that they are a waste of time; that it is hard to make yourself heard; that emotions run too high; and that meetings impinge upon 'real' work. This does not have to be the case – following a few simple guidelines will make meetings the ideal forum for whole groups to communicate.

When to Call a Meeting

Only call a meeting when it is absolutely necessary. Meetings are time specific, and they may involve travel. Call a meeting when:

- there is a lot to be discussed.

- the issues are complex.

- the input of several people is needed.

- visual aids or props are required.

How to Handle a Meeting

Use precise times

Be rigid about the timing of the meeting: inform the others that the meeting will start, and conclude, at the appointed times.

Minimise the length
You shouldn't allow more than two hours for a meeting; one hour is even better. If more than two hours is needed, consider calling two separate meetings. At the very least, have a break in the middle.

Set an agenda
Have a clear agenda, and send this out – as a memo or letter, rather than a fax or email – well in advance. This will give people time to prepare their thoughts or to collect any information they may need.

Appoint a chair
The chairperson must be an individual who is more concerned with making sure that everyone has their say and understands the issues than making their own opinions heard.

Take minutes
Ensure that somebody takes minutes of the meeting, so that there is a written record of what has been said. The minutes should subsequently be sent out to all present at the meeting, so that everyone has a shared understanding of what went on. The person who takes the minutes can vary, if the group so wishes, with each meeting.

6. Communicating – in Presentations

Learning to communicate effectively in presentations is a demanding skill, but one that can be mastered.

> Make a slide or an overhead with the main topics listed and put a box next to each one. As each topic is completed, show this slide, and tick off the corresponding box. This will ensure a smooth transition from one topic to the next and allows the audience to grasp the relevance and context of each point you are making.

Step 1: Prepare visual aids
Your audience will be impressed if you prepare overheads, slides, handouts or posters to accompany your talk. This will demonstrate that you have a great deal of knowledge about your subject and want to present it in the best manner possible. It also shows that you have taken time to prepare, which always impresses; and using visual aids can transform a dull talk into a lively and interesting presentation by varying the way in which the audience receives their information (visual as opposed to just aural).

Starting off by asking a rhetorical question is always a good way to gain the attention of the audience.

- Make sure that the room you are using has the appropriate equipment. It is always a good idea to check in advance with your host.

- Ensure that the text, pictures or overheads are large enough for the audience to see. Text should be at least 20 point-size; preferably 30.

- Don't clutter the material with too much information. A few bullet points per slide or overhead is adequate.

- Bullet points and short lists are ideal for displaying information in a digestible manner.

- Always read out what is on your slides.

- Only use visuals that directly support the message – don't provide unnecessary or distracting material.

- Point to the part of the visual to which you are referring.

- Don't keep the visual on display longer than necessary or put it up before you have reached that point in your presentation.

- Some people feel that use of colour is unprofessional. Others believe that using two or three colours enhances your presentation, especially if the colour is used to highlight certain points.

- Ensure that all your slides or overheads are in the correct order and that they are organised and accessible. It is a good idea to put them in transparent wallets – the sort suitable for overhead projection – which can be placed and replaced in a ringbinder.

Most people decide very quickly, just seconds into a speech, whether to accept or reject what is being said. [Source: Hall, 1959]
   The introduction is crucial. A good introduction should:

- introduce yourself and your credentials (if necessary).

- tell the audience what the presentation is about.

- tell the audience what they will gain from the presentation.

- preview and lead to the main area of the speech.

The conclusion to your presentation is equally important. Always end with what is called 'a satisfying closure'. [Source: Fisher, 1993] Summarise the main points of your talk and, if appropriate, indicate the next step for either you or for the audience. If you want them to take action in any way, now is the time to say so. If you are going to follow up with an update in six weeks' time, tell them this as well.

Step 2: Prepare and practice
- Prepare notes on index cards, even if they are just keywords to prompt you. Alternatively, you can print these keywords on your overheads.

- Make a confident entrance – walk up to the rostrum with assured steps.

- Speak slowly, audibly and clearly.

- Pause to let people take in information.

- Make eye contact with people as you talk.

- Tell the audience what you are going to say at the beginning. At the end, reiterate what you've told them.

- Face the audience. Many people end up talking to the blackboard, flipchart or slide and their words become lost.

- Stand straight and tall.

Step 3: Dealing with nerves

The main cause of nervousness before a presentation is uncertainty or lack of confidence; the more prepared you are, the less anxious you will be.

If you are feeling unbearably tense and nervous, try a few deep breathing exercises. Breathe in through your nose, hold for a few seconds, and exhale slowly through your mouth. With each breath, try to relax a different muscle, until you are feeling more calm.

Try asking yourself what is the worst thing that could happen to you; attempt to put your fears into perspective. Remind yourself that there is no reason why this shouldn't be a good and interesting presentation – after all, people don't want to see you trip up; they want to learn something from what you have to say.

When a US study asked 2500 Americans what they were most scared of, over 40 per cent said 'Speaking before a group'. The other statistics were as follows:

- heights: 30%

- insects: 22.1%

- financial problems: 22%

- deep water: 21.5%

- sickness: 18.8%

- death: 18.7%

- flying: 18.3%

- loneliness: 13.6%

- dogs: 11.2%

[Multiple responses were given]

[Source: Wallechinsky and Wallace, 1977]

Step 4: Answering questions

Something else that often induces anxiety is the possibility of being asked questions – particularly those to which you do not know the answer.

- Always repeat the question for the benefit of those who may not have heard it.

- Thank the questioner for the question, and add how glad you are that it was brought up.

- Address your answer primarily to the questioner, but sweep your gaze around the rest of the audience as well. Make them feel included; it is not a private conversation between you and the questioner.

- Ensure that the questioner is satisfied with your response.

- If you don't know the answer, don't panic. Thank the questioner and say:

  "I'm not sure of the answer; but it is an extremely good point, and I'm going to check it out immediately."

  Alternatively, throw the question back to the individual, or to the rest of the audience, and see if they know.

Golden Rule

The key to effective presentation is confidence. Remember: if you act confidently, you will appear – and eventually feel – confident.

---

7. Communicating – without Words

What is NVC?

Non-verbal communication (NVC) is the silent means by which we communicate, either intentionally or unconsciously, also referred to as 'body language'.

Intentional NVC would include, for example, the thumbs-up signal given in many cultures to indicate pleasure or agreement.

Unconscious NVC would include the way in which the pupils of our eyes dilate if we are happy or excited, and contract when we are unhappy or bored.

What conveys NVC?

- Facial expressions.

- Gestures.

- The position of our arms and legs.

- Posture.

- Voice characteristics: tone of voice, pitch of voice, volume, and the rate at which we speak.

Facial Expressions

The face is the most expressive part of the body. It consists of a huge number of muscles allowing us to use varying combinations of eye, mouth, forehead and even nose movements to convey different expressions.

The face is capable of producing 250,000 different expressions. [Source: Birdwhistell, 1970]

Expression Management

Humans have a unique capacity to be able to display emotions that we don't feel inside. We open an unwanted gift in front of the giver and proffer a huge smile; we adopt a neutral expression on hearing that we have been passed over for promotion.

Our faces, then, can – and should – be used to create the impression that is desired, expected and necessary to succeed at work, whatever our internal state may be. Your ultimate aim should be to detect someone else's true feelings through their facial expressions, while at the same time managing yourself to convey the correct impression.

 SEE CHAPTER 1

What the Face Says

Facial Expression	What it Implies
Wide smile; crinkling around the eyes.	Genuine pleasure or warmth.
Wide smile, not reaching eyes.	Faked pleasure.
Eyes open wide and mouth open.	Genuine surprise.
Eyes open wide or mouth open.	Faked surprise.
Eyes flickering around room rather than at other person.	Disinterest, boredom – even dishonesty.
Large pupils.	Interest, excitement, liking.
Small pupils.	Disinterest, dislike, boredom.
Suppressed yawn.	Boredom.
Un-suppressed yawn.	Probably genuine fatigue.

Arm and Leg Positions

Limb Position	What it Means
Folded arms.	Boredom, disinterest, even hostility.
One arm by side, the other one across front (or back) of body gripping the elbow.	Lack of confidence, nervousness.
Hands on hips or waist.	Defensiveness or aggression.
Standing up with legs crossed at knees.	Defensiveness (if arms are crossed, too) or disinterest.
Leaning one hand on door or wall.	'I am trying to intimidate you'.

Gestures

Gestures can be used to emphasise a statement; alternatively – if you know what to look for – they can contradict what is being said.

What the gestures say

Gesture	What it Implies
Elbow on the desk, one thumb under the chin and a finger on the cheek.	Interest.
Leaning forward in chair slightly, hands together and interlocking.	Interest.
Tapping with fingers.	Irritation, impatience or nervousness.
Repetitive movement of foot.	Boredom or impatience.
Putting fingers of both hands together to make a 'steeple'.	Confidence or superiority.
Covering mouth.	There is something to hide.
Touching neck or nose.	Lying.
Rubbing eyes.	Lying (or tiredness).
Rubbing or touching ear.	Possibly a signal that the gesturer does not want to hear any more.
Scratching neck.	Disagreement.
Stroking chin.	Deep thought or contemplation.
Pulling collar.	Lying.
Occasional nodding.	'Continue speaking'.
Rapid nodding.	'Stop speaking – I want to speak'.

Posture

Posture is fairly easy to interpret, but you should not read one NVC sign in isolation.

Example:

A relaxed posture may suggest a relaxed manner, but an individual who can properly read NVC will notice the foot tapping that 'leaks' the real emotion of boredom.

Mirroring

People tend to subconsciously copy, or 'mirror', others' posture when they like or agree with them. Take advantage of this: deliberately mirror (within reason) the person you are trying to impress. They will subconsciously pick up on the signal that you agree with them.

Voice characteristics

The meaning of a message can be subtly altered by changing the pitch and speed of the voice, or by including laughter, groans, whines and coughs.

Voice Characteristic	What it (could) Mean
Loud voice.	I want you to get the message; and/or I am the boss.
Soft voice.	I want you to think I am warm and friendly (look for other signs to find out if this is genuine).
Very quiet voice.	I am not confident; and/or I do not believe in what I am saying.
High, squeaky voice.	I am defensive or excited.
Rapid speech.	I am excited and enthusiastic.

Chapter Checkpoint

After reading this chapter, you should:

- know why communication is important.
- know the basics of successful telephone communication.
- understand when and how to use email.
- have learned when and how to use letters, faxes and memos.
- know how to make the best use of meetings.
- have learned the basics of giving a presentation.
- understand all the varying forms of non-verbal communication.

In the Next Chapter

How to cope with stress at work.

Further Reading

Evans, D. W., *Communication at Work: An Introduction to Business Communication and Information* (London: Pitman Publishing, 1987).

Siegman, A. W., *Non-verbal Behavior and Communication* (New Jersey: L. Erlbaum, 1986).

Knapp, M., *Essentials of Non-verbal Communication* (London: Holt, Rienhardt and Winston, 1980).

Smithson, S., *Business Communication Today: A Guide to Effective Communication Techniques* (Cambridge: ICSA, 1984).

Chapter Seven

Take It Easy: Coping with Stress at Work

The Aim

Career advancement – tackle the tension, take control of your stress, move smoothly through the day.

"Stress is the scourge of the modern world. It is impossible not to be stressed – I think most of us walk around in a perpetual state of stress and there seems to be little that can be done about it."

Tom, Managing Editor

"Stress is the result of having too much to do and not enough time to do it in. I am always rushing round like a headless chicken, but never feel that I am winning."

Yasmin, Accountant

"I get stressed when I am trying to juggle my work commitments, my home-life, my partner, my kids, parents... and still find time for a social life! If only there was twice as much time – I'm sure that would reduce my stress levels."

Azmeh, Sales Representative

"I prefer to work under some stress. I am in a very deadline-oriented industry and am always working my socks off to meet one deadline or other. After each one, I pretty much collapse, and often come down with a cold or something."

Eric, Journalist

Most of us feel stressed at some time or other; some people become so stressed that they fall ill. Many people try and ignore their stress levels, believing that if they work harder their company will benefit. In actual fact, ignoring stress is unlikely to benefit your company: huge amounts of money are lost through stress-related illness, and studies have also shown that work performance falls rapidly when stress rises to high levels. [Source: Baron, 1986]

As the opening comments show, attitudes to stress vary from person to person. Some people thrive on it; others seem to collapse at the first sign of strain. There is subsequently no prescribed formula for dealing with stress – the trick is to find techniques that help you.

What is universally true about stress, however, is that it has become a prominent feature of modern life. It is vital that you understand the signs, causes and effects of stress, and – most importantly – how to deal with this twentieth-century malaise.

To deal successfully with stress, you must first understand exactly what it is. You should then assess your own stress levels, and look at the possible causes of acute or chronic anxiety.

Having established these basics, you will be able to use one or more of several different strategies to minimise your stress. The approach chosen should depend primarily on the source of anxiety, and on what is best for you in terms of your lifestyle and personality.

Stress does not come purely from external sources, however. Your personality plays a large part in how stressed you will become. If you understand what elements of your personality encourage stress, you can attempt to replace them with different, and less stress-inducing, behaviour.

The path to a successful career will always be paved with some stress; coping with it will keep you moving smoothly and swiftly upwards to your goal.

It is estimated that nearly 10 per cent of the UK's Gross National Product is lost each year due to stress in the form of factors such as sickness absence, lost production and reduced quality of work. [Source: Cooper and Robertson, 1998]

1. Stress – What Is It?

'Stress' – a word derived from the Latin *stringere*, 'to draw tight'; conjuring up images of tension, anxiety, inability to cope, pressure, strain, lack of control, powerlessness, fatigue and distress.

Most of the above are in fact the symptoms of stress, rather than the thing itself. Stress is actually a perfectly normal reaction to events around us, and is a throwback to our evolutionary history. For our ancestors, the stress reaction was essential for survival, a coping mechanism that provided extra reserves of strength and energy, to facilitate an escape from whatever predator was considering them for supper.

Our Bodies: Fleeing, Fighting and Releasing Hormones

In 1939 a psychologist called Cannon revealed that stress is a 'flight or fight' mechanism; a device which prepares our body either to stay and fight the source of fear (a large predator, for example), or to run for the hills. [Source: Cannon, 1939]

The physician Hans Selye made an early scientific attempt to explain the stress reaction as a three-part General Adaptation Syndrome:

Stage 1: Alarm Reaction. The individual's defence mechanism becomes active.

Stage 2: Resistance. The body learns to cope with the stress by increasing its defences.

Stage 3: Exhaustion. Eventually, if the stress is not removed, the body will go into the exhaustion stage.

[Source: Selye, 1946]

Stage 1: Alarm Reaction

When we are stressed, hormones are released from the adrenal glands into the bloodstream, with the aim of preparing the body for flight or fight. Fighting and fleeing both require extra strength in the arms and legs, and more energy in the muscles. The aim is to divert as much oxygen- (energy-) carrying blood as possible to the arm and leg muscles. The body therefore stops concentrating on the non-essential functions like digestion, and blood is diverted from the stomach, skin and internal organs to other more important areas.

One of the hormones released is *adrenaline*: it leads to a faster heart rate and raised blood pressure, as the heart works harder to pump blood around the body.

Cortisol is another hormone released from the adrenal glands, and its function is to act on the liver converting protein to glucose (sugar): a major source of energy. The glucose helps the blood to be pumped more quickly, allowing us to run or fight with extra strength.

Endorphins are released from the hypothalamus in the brain. They act as natural pain-killers, enabling us to concentrate on the situation in hand.

Stages 2 and 3: The Problems

The 'alarm reaction' was ideal for our ancestors, who would thus be perfectly prepared for a vicious fight with (or flight from) an angry predator. These days the threat is much more likely to be a deadline, an angry boss or demanding children than a wild lion, and this is where the 'alarm reaction' falls down. Threat-response mechanisms have not adapted well to the modern stresses of the twentieth and twenty-first centuries.

The 'alarm reaction' is thus far less necessary in our society, which leads to Stages 2 and 3 of stress.

Stage 2 is the short-term effect – *resistance*. What happens to all the hormones, glucose and energy if they are not being used in flight or fight?

Stage 3 is the long-term effect – *exhaustion*. What happens if our bodies are continually being bombarded with hormones and chemicals?

Stage 2: Short-term Effects (Resistance)

The excess amount of glucose and hormones surging through our muscles with nowhere to go can result in a variety of different symptoms.

Symptom	Cause
Aching limbs	The build-up of glucose in the limbs can make the arms and legs feel heavy and tired. In addition, the muscles are tensed in preparation for flight or fight and this tension causes pain.
Headache	An increase in blood supply to the brain enables clear thinking, but a build-up causes headaches.
Neck ache	The neck muscles are tensed, causing pain.
Tiredness	The burning-up of extra energy inevitably causes tiredness.
Dry mouth	The flow of saliva to the mouth is reduced.
Stomach ache or butterflies	Blood is diverted away from this area and the digestive mechanisms are reduced leading possibly to digestive problems, and discomfort.
Dizziness	When stressed, we tend to take more shallow breaths. This can lead to a slightly reduced oxygen supply to the brain, causing dizziness.

Stage 3: Long-term effects (Exhaustion)

Prolonged stress also has a variety of effects upon a person.

Condition	Cause
Hypertension (raised blood pressure); coronary heart disease	Hypertension is caused by a continually raised heart rate. Raised heart rate can also cause a rapid build-up of cholesterol by increasing small lesions on the artery walls, which trap cholesterol. This may lead eventually to a narrowing of the arteries, and to coronary heart disease.
Stomach ulcers	Poor digestion over prolonged periods can result in stomach problems. In addition, there will be an excess of acid in the stomach, which could lead to stomach ulcers.
Exhaustion	This is caused by a rapid mobilisation of energy, giving short-term benefits, but resulting in long-term exhaustion.
Skin disorders	Rashes and allergies may be caused by the continued decrease in blood supply to the skin.
Frequent colds or flu	Stress can result in a lowered immune system, making the person more vulnerable to disease.

Coronary heart disease is the leading cause of death in the UK, and over half of all Americans die of cardiovascular disease. [Source: Cooper and Robertson, 1998]

2. Are You Stressed?

You may not have all the symptoms of stress at any one time, but if you have any of them for any length of time, consider preventative measures – now.

The Stress Test

Analyse your stress levels now with this quick test.

On a piece of paper write down, on a scale of 1–5, how much each of the following statements has applied to you over the last three months.

- **1: Very frequently.**
- **2: Frequently.**
- **3: Sometimes.**
- **4: Infrequently.**
- **5: Very infrequently, never.**

I eat more or less than I usually do.

I suffer from indigestion or heartburn.

I suffer from constipation, stomach aches, diarrhoea or other stomach problems.

I suffer from sleep problems – for example, difficulty getting to sleep or waking up early.

I feel tired or exhausted.

I have headaches.

I feel like crying, or as if I might 'explode'.

I can't sit still without fidgeting, or I pace the floor, and so on.

I feel my heart rate increasing, and worry about my blood pressure.

I get impatient or irritable easily.

I feel unable to cope.

I have difficulty making decisions.

I have difficulty concentrating.

I move on to the next task before completing the present task.

I smoke more or drink more alcohol than I used to.

I worry about so many things.

I feel tense not relaxed.

I feel that I don't have time for everything.

I feel panicky or fearful.

Now add up your score.

20–40: Very high stress

40–60: High stress

60–80: Mild stress

80–100: Low stress

A Note on Acute vs. Chronic Stress

Sometimes, people find themselves under 'acute' stress which means that the levels of tension are building, but that the stress under which they find themselves is essentially short-term. Chronic stress, by contrast, is caused by a build-up of tension over a long period of time.

More than 80

Your stress levels appear to be reasonably under control and you do not seem to be suffering too many symptoms of long-term stress. However, even if you do not consciously feel stressed, there are some danger signs to watch out for.

If you are suffering from acute stress you may occasionally feel impatient, irritable or tense during your working day. Further indications are an inability to relax, even after work. Some people use artificial means in order to help them to relax, such as alcohol.

Less than 80; more than 60

You are suffering from mild stress. This is an early warning sign. Some stress can be healthy, but when you start experiencing physical and emotional symptoms like those listed above you should start finding ways to reduce it.

Less than 60; more than 40

You are stressed: you don't simply feel occasionally tense, your stress has been building up over at least the last three months. You probably feel constantly tired, have sleeping difficulties, are impatient and irritable, are always trying to do too much, and feel that there is simply not time to do everything.

Take stock of the situation, and take steps to reduce your stress now.

There are several ways to do this. Most bookshops and libraries stock a wide variety of self-help books and it might be worthwhile obtaining one of these. Alternatively, see a stress counsellor (usually listed in the *Yellow Pages*). Stress counsellors are more expensive, but will provide a programme tailored to your needs. Or you could see your GP, who will also suggest various remedies to you – and who will see people like you every single day.

You will also find further advice on combating stress later in this chapter.

Less than 40

Your stress levels are very high: take action now.

Chronic stress can raise your blood pressure and lower your immunity, exposing you to the risk of colds, flu and minor infections. In the long-term you increase your susceptibility to hypertension and coronary heart disease. In other words, your lifestyle is unhealthy. It is likely to be even less healthy if you smoke, do not take exercise and eat poor quality meals.

Once again, refer to the advice above to begin reducing your stress levels.

3. Stressed – Why?

In order to reduce your levels of stress, you must first identify what is causing it: the stressors in your life.

The Stress Diary

Firstly, keep a 'stress diary' for two weeks. It can be filled in either throughout the day, or at the end of each day.

Within the stress diary the following should be recorded:

- an incident that made you feel stressed.

- a score of 0–100 of how stressed you felt (where 0 = no stress and 100 = the most stressed you have ever felt).

- a description of the symptoms, sensations or feelings you experienced.

- how long these symptoms lasted.

- what – if anything – happened to make you feel better.

Here is an example of how your diary might look:

Date/Time	Incident	Score	Symptoms	Outcome
March 26th, 10 a.m.	Boss returned a report to me, indicating that parts needed re-doing.	60	I felt panicky because I just didn't have the time to re-do it. I felt out of control, powerless and that I just couldn't do anything. Wanted to cry or run away. After a bit, I developed a headache.	I worked till midnight on the report and felt better when I went to bed.
March 27th, 4.30 p.m.	My car wouldn't start.	80	Felt angry and upset at once. Felt that the world was against me and that everything always goes wrong – why me? Heart was pounding, neck started to ache. I started thinking about all the things I had to do.	Rang a friend who came and jump-started the car. My feelings never really subsided and I couldn't sleep that night for worrying about everything.
March 28th, 5 p.m.	No one incident.	60	My stress had been building all day – I spent the day running from one thing to another. First, I tore around the supermarket, then rushed back to take Katie to ballet, then rushed to cook for a dinner party. By late afternoon, I needed a strong gin just to calm myself down.	The alcohol relaxed me enough not to care if the dinner party wasn't perfect.

Reading through your stress diary, decide which of the categories below are the main sources of your tension. Beneath each category you will find details of one or more 'strategies': these refer to a later section in this chapter that deals with stress-reduction techniques. You will find the strategies mentioned particularly helpful in dealing with that specific situation.

Workload

Most people assume that too much work is stressful, and are surprised to learn that too little is also a source of stress. In both cases, it is the inability to do anything about the pace which contributes to the stress. Further, a heavy workload does not necessarily mean that the worker is sufficiently challenged: the tasks may be numerous but the work can still be monotonous, providing little job satisfaction.

Strategies: 1, 2, 6 and 7

Long Hours

Working late into the night to finish projects impacts on personal and family life, leaving the demands from these areas to increase. Shopping, washing and other chores build up, while pressure – and resentment – from family members mounts up. Not only that, the opportunities for stress-reducing activities like hobbies or going out are reduced.

Strategies: 1, 2, 6 and 7

Job Insecurity

These days, job insecurity is a factor of almost everybody's career. The days of the job for life are long gone, the fear of becoming unemployed is ever-present, and constantly worrying about your future is inherently stressful.

Strategies: 1, 2, 3 and 4

Responsibility

Responsibility for the welfare, work and safety of other people is a significant source of stress, as is responsibility for budgets or equipment. People may find themselves continually worrying about their responsibilities, and unable to switch off their concerns at the end of the day.

Studies in the 1960s found that responsibility for people was far more stressful than responsibility for things.
[Source: Wardwell, Hyman and Bahnson, 1964]

On the other hand, just as too little work can cause stress, so can too little responsibility.

Strategies: 1, 2, 5 and 6

Change

The world is changing ever more quickly and never more so than in the world of work. As companies struggle to stay afloat in a changing economy, they seek new ways of working and structuring the workforce to meet the changing climate. Mergers and acquisitions are rife, as are such processes as 'delayering', 'business process re-engineering', 'empowerment' and other concepts all indicating the same thing – change and uncertainty.

Strategies: 1, 2, 3, 4 and 5

Life Events

Certain life events are significant sources of stress. Some are negative, like the death of a family member; some are positive, like moving house or getting married.

In each case, it takes time to adjust to the new circumstances, and each event will invariably involve extra demands on time, energy and emotions. If the stressful events occur at a time when stress levels are already high, coping can be quite a challenge, and it can be very hard not to let this affect your performance at work.

Strategies: 1, 2, 3 and 4

Family and Friends

Stress can occur when partners, family or friends object either to the job itself or to aspects such as the hours. Further tension can occur when those around us make demands for time or attention that conflict with other needs such as hobbies.

Strategies: 1, 2, 5, 6 and 7

The Work Environment
Noise
One of the most common problems of the workplace is unwanted sound or noise, caused either by machinery, by the noise of ringing phones or by colleagues talking loudly. Such noise may well disrupt concentration and cause headaches.

The worker usually has no control over such noise, which is the main psychological factor in turning unwanted sound into an irritant. If the individual had control over the volume, even if they didn't turn it down, the noise would be better tolerated.
Strategies: 1 and 5

Temperature
Being too hot or too cold in the office can be a source of stress as well. As with unwanted noise, the concentration can be impaired while the lack of control is demotivating. Poor or inadequate lighting can have the same result.
Strategies 1 and 5

Space
The issue of personal space can also become stressful. Humans are territorial and we like to have space that we can call our own. When others invade that space we can become tense and anxious; thus, in open-plan offices, workers often improvise dividers with books or screens.

The worst kind of environment has to be the latest trend of 'hot-desking' where workers do not have any personal space at all: they arrive at work and take whatever desk they can find. These work environments are used more for teleworkers, and can be stressful for those involved despite claims that such an atmosphere is egalitarian and liberating.
Strategies 1 and 5

> **One researcher has claimed that 'poor mental health [is] directly related to unpleasant working conditions'.** [Source: Kornhauser, 1965]

Relationships at Work
Rivalry, back-stabbing, gossip, jibes, nasty comments – all sources of work stress. Not only do poor relationships with other colleagues cause tension and anxiety, but they also eliminate an important source of stress reduction: mutual support.

The necessity of getting on with a team can cause tension while group pressure to conform can be similarly stressful, especially if the dissenter is convinced that the others are wrong.

SEE CHAPTER 4
Strategies: 1, 2 and 5

Role Stress
Stress is often caused by demands on an individual to play two or more conflicting roles, or by ambiguity about which role to take on under what circumstances. The person may be asked to do something that they know will displease someone else, or may be expected to do tasks not within their job remit or which conflict with their ideology. Stress is caused by the inability to meet these expectations and demands.

Tension is also caused by a desire to perform tasks in a manner different to that sanctioned by the company. Further role ambiguity can occur if an employee is not told how to perform their job or if they are not sure what is expected of them – a common problem for those in their first job, a new job or a promotion.

SEE CHAPTER 4

Strategies: 1, 2, 5 and 7

Information Overload

From the moment we wake up we are continually bombarded with information. The backs of our cereal packets tell us about great prizes to be won, the television blares out the news, advertising hoardings tell of new products, our mail is full of correspondence and junk... even our faxes and emails continually disgorge large quantities of information. Many of us also subscribe to magazines and newspapers.

Feeling unable to cope with all the information we need to read, then, is inevitable. We end up moving pieces of paper from one in-tray to another, becoming more and more stressed as we struggle to read and absorb everything.

Strategies: 1, 3, 4 and 7

Shift Work

The problems of shift work are both physical and psychological. Physically, night shifts disturb the biological (circadian) rhythms. These rhythms regulate our sleep/wake cycle and are also responsible for our patterns of digestion, and body temperature regulation. When these are disrupted, especially our sleeping patterns, we are likely to feel irritable and stressed – the effects of jet-lag are very similar.

> **The physician Hans Selye once suggested that learning to live with, and get along with, other people is one of life's most stressful aspects.** [Source: Selye, 1974]

Psychologically, if the worker has little control over the shifts they work, this may also be a source of stress.

The best shift patterns to work are either very rapidly changing ones (one night on, one night off) or two-week shifts. In the first case the circadian rhythms do not need to change, while in the second, the rhythms have enough time between the different shifts to adjust.

Strategies: 1, 6 and 7

Travel

Travel is stressful, especially during rush-hour. 'Road-rage' can result from the pent-up stress and frustration of traffic jams, while a lack of control over the situation is again a factor. The extra vigilance required when travelling in bad conditions can be another source of stress, especially for the tired worker at the end of the day.

Strategies: 1, 6 and 7.

4. Strategies for Dealing with Stress

You now know what stress is, how stressed you are, and what the source of your stress is. Time now to do something about it.

The solution isn't quick and easy – you will need to put effort and energy into reducing and managing your stress.

Since everyone is different and each person has different stressors, a number of varying strategies are listed below. You can select a few, or just one. You may adopt three for a few months, and try a different set later on. The only important thing is that the stress is reduced.

Strategy One: Prevention – Better Than Cure

One of the best ways to deal with stress is to see it coming, and to deal with it before it happens. Short-term strategies for dealing with stressful situations include:

- talking. To your friends, your partner – even the dog. Just getting things off your chest will help to get them into perspective.

- making time for yourself. Whatever your chosen method of unwinding is – having a bath, having a massage, aromatherapy or simply watching television – do it. And don't feel guilty, either: making time to do the things you like doing is vital if you want to remain happy and motivated at work.

- find an outside pursuit which has nothing to do with your working, or home, environment. Yoga, t'ai chi, amateur dramatics, belly-dancing... whatever. Just as long as it remains a part of your life that is both enjoyable and separate to work.

Sometimes, however, it just happens. Things get on top of you, the pressure mounts, and before you know it you feel completely strung-out, tense, unable to unwind or enjoy yourself any more. Time now to look at some long-term strategies to deal with your chronic stress – strategies that, given time and patience, will almost certainly reduce your stress levels significantly.

Strategy Two: Relaxation

There are a number of options here. The most extensive (and expensive) option is to find a relaxation therapist who will guide you through a series of relaxation exercises over a period of time. Try the *Yellow Pages*.

The second option is to buy a book on relaxation techniques – most good bookshops will stock such books.

The third option is to buy one of many relaxation tapes that will guide you through a 'Deep Relaxation' process. Such tapes can often be found in specialist bookshops – again, consult your *Yellow Pages*.

There is no doubt that 'Deep Relaxation', as this particular technique is called, is extremely effective for many people. Such a tape should be used on a daily basis, and usually requires a time commitment of about 30 minutes a day, at least for the first few weeks of use (the tape may tell you how and when to reduce the time spent practising Deep Relaxation).

Used effectively, Deep Relaxation will lower your blood pressure, slow down your breathing and reduce the amount of adrenaline in your blood. [Source: Matteson and Ivancevich, 1987] One study which used Deep Muscle Relaxation as part of a stress management programme found that blood pressure was reduced after just six sessions. [Source: Tisdelle, Hansen, St Lawrence and Brown, 1984]

Strategy Three: Thought-Catching

'If I could only stop those niggling worries circling round my mind, surely I'd be much less stressed...'

It can be done. The 'thought-catching' technique advocated by many clinical psychologists is useful in preventing continual worrying. It revolves around the concepts of training and habit-breaking, and can be extremely effective.

Thought-catching

When you next worry, write down the thought. Next to this 'stressor', write down as many connected thoughts as you can: why you are worried, what could happen, and so on.

Think about the connected thoughts — are they rational? Are they realistic? In the next column, write down more positive thoughts: how you can overcome the concern, how you could get help to deal with it, and so on.

After about three weeks of this you should be able to 'catch' your thoughts in your head without having to write them down.

'Caught' Thought	Negative Thoughts	Positive Thoughts
I am worried that I will not finish my report on time.	My boss will be disappointed in me. I will not get promoted. I may even get fired. I will feel that I have let my boss down.	If I ask my partner to take on some of the chores, I could work through the next two evenings to get it finished. This will be the first time I have given a report in late. My boss is not really likely to fire me — they will understand that I am overworked.
I am stressed because I have no time for anything anymore.	Everything is getting on top of me. I hardly have time to breathe. The stress is making me ill.	I'll make a list of everything I want to do. I'll prioritise the list. I'll learn to say 'no' to the things I don't want to do. I'll ask my boss for some administrative help to take some of my load off.

Strategy Four: Worry-Periods

Most concerns are long-term and will not disappear, so constant worrying all day will only wear you down. Try using the 'worry-period' technique to have as much freedom from worry as possible.

Allow a set period for worrying – say 30 minutes a day – at a set time. Any worrying may only be done during that period. During the worry-period, you may sweat over your concerns as much as you like, as you try and decide how you will handle each one. Then it's time-up until the next day's worry-period.

If any worries pop into your head during the day they should be noted on paper and saved for the worry-period. You can refer back to them later.

The Day's Worries

8.30 a.m.:	work appraisal next week
8.40 a.m.:	elderly parents
9.10 a.m.:	work appraisal
9.20 a.m.:	too much work
9.45 a.m.:	too much work
10.10 a.m.:	health concern
11.20 a.m.:	too much work
11.45 a.m.:	when will I do the shopping?
12.20 p.m.:	elderly parents
12.45 p.m.:	my future and career
1.10 p.m.:	work appraisal

And so on.

Many of this worrier's thoughts recur frequently, and most are connected with their job. In the worry-period, therefore, this worrier should think about:

• their job.

• whether they can do anything about the overwork.

• whether they can prepare for the appraisal.

• whether they should look for a different job.

• whether they should go to a doctor with the health issue.

• possible care options for their elderly parents.

Strategy Five: Assertion

"My problem is that when anyone asks me to do anything, I always like to say 'yes'. It can be the boss, colleagues, my partner, friends... whoever it is, I hate to say no. I don't really know why... I think it is because I like to please and I feel guilty if I turn people down. I also like to think that I am capable and can do anything. If I say 'no', then people might think I can't cope. Or maybe it is me who will think I can't cope."

Aaron, Social Worker

Aaron takes on far too much, gets immensely stressed, and subsequently spends most of his waking moments worrying about how to get everything done. He has difficulty sleeping and rarely has time for socialising or even eating properly. If this sounds familiar, assertion techniques could work for you.

SEE CHAPTER 8

Strategy Six: Exercise

Exercise encourages an overall lowering of blood pressure and steadier breathing, and can counteract the physical consequences of stress. If you exercise frequently, your blood pressure will not rise so much during periods of stress, protecting you from symptoms like hypertension and coronary heart disease. Fit individuals may also be less 'psychologically reactive' in stressful situations – in other words, they would be less likely to react in a psychological manner by becoming anxious, depressed and so on. [Source: Sutherland and Cooper, 1993] Exercising during times of stress will also use up excess energy in a positive way. [Source: Falkenberg, 1987] The best form of exercise to take is aerobic and examples of aerobic exercise include jogging, walking and swimming. Sports such as tennis or squash are also useful for releasing tension and energy.

Strategy Seven: Learning the Art of Time Management

Read the following list, and make a note of your agreement or disagreement with each statement.

I have too much to do.
I could delegate, but I tend to do things myself.
I feel that I never have time to think.
I get too involved in details and spend ages on them.
I delay doing things and procrastinate a lot.
I always have unexpected visitors, or visitors who stay too long.
I have too many telephone interruptions.
I waste too much time in meetings.
I don't really have clear objectives and goals.
I hate saying 'no'.
I am not very good at prioritising.
I am always troubleshooting rather than taking preventative action.
Paperwork and administration takes up too much time.
I work a lot of evenings and weekends.
I have difficulty meeting deadlines.
I don't spend much time planning future work.

If you agree with more than five of the statements, you should be attempting to manage your time more effectively.

Prioritise

Make a list of all the things you need to do, complete with their deadlines. Mark them 1–5 for priority, and strike off each task from the list when it is completed. When you have more than one job at the same priority level do the most unpleasant jobs first to avoid procrastination. Always avoid trying to do more than one thing at a time.

Task	Deadline	Priority (1 = most important)
Write article	21 April	1
Prepare presentation	25 April	1
Visit parents	None	4
Paint spare room	None	4
Design magazine cover	May	3

Delegate

Delegate wherever possible. At work, give tasks when you can to subordinates or administrators, and outsource if you can.

(At home, try paying someone to do the ironing, or have a cleaner come once a week, if you can afford it.)

Discourage interruptions

Display a recognised symbol or sign at work to demonstrate a desire not to be interrupted, and allow your answerphone or voice mail to take messages in order to finish a task.

Be organised

Don't waste time trying to find memos, notes, phone numbers or lists. Use one large desk diary and have sections in it with 'to do' lists, 'calls to make', and so on. Have a wall calendar so that you can see at a glance what needs to be done and when.

Be realistic

Do not under-estimate how long a task will take – it is better to be realistic, and to over-estimate. Similarly, build in 'what-if' time to your schedule, allowing extra time to cover unforeseen circumstances. Having decided your time limit, stick to it.

Maximise meetings

Time wasted in meetings can be reduced by:

- ensuring that each meeting is really necessary.
- starting and finishing on time.
- cutting out interruptions.
- having an efficient and organised chairperson.

Be at your best...

Find out when you work best: some people are 'owls', who work best in the evening; others are 'larks' who are at their most alert in the morning. Do the most important and demanding jobs when you are normally at your best.

...But avoid being 'the best'

A perfectionist is a person who does not know when to stop working on a task, call it completed, and move on to another. Do things well, but know when to call a task finished.

5. Emotion Management

A significant source of stress at work is also likely to come from the mental effort of having to control or manage the emotional front that you present. Emotion management may be necessary because you are worried or upset about something in your personal life (for example, financial worries, health concerns or relationship difficulties), or because of something that may have happened at work itself (a customer may have been rude to you, your boss may have been aggressive or a colleague dismissive).

In all the above situations we usually try to hide our true feelings and put on a 'brave face'. After all, we might not want others to know about our personal problems, or to admit that we are upset by a colleague. In many work environments, especially those that are 'customer facing', workers are simply not allowed to do anything other than smile sweetly at customers, when what they really want to do is scream at them.

How to Cope

Learn to act...

Emotion management is part of the skill of Impression Management, whereby we learn to create and maintain an impression for an audience. If you can mask negative emotions and maintain a professional front, people will respect you more.

SEE CHAPTER 1

...But not all the time

Make sure that you have the opportunity to release your true emotions. Failure to find this release could be stressful, and may contribute towards you feeling burntout and emotionally exhausted.

Talk it out

Find someone you can talk to about how you really feel – this could be a trusted colleague, a spouse or partner, or even a mentor.

Write it down

It can be cathartic to write down your real feelings – but if you do this at work, make sure that you keep your jottings safe from prying eyes.

Acceptance and understanding

Acknowledge that managing emotions is stressful, and if you are going through a particularly bad time it is often acceptable to tell colleagues, and to ask them to make allowances should your 'mask' slip during the day.

6. Reviewing Your Personality

Of course, not all stress comes from external sources. Your stress levels do, to a considerable extent, depend on how you personally handle various situations and your attitude to life generally.

Read the following list and make a note of your agreement or disagreement with each statement.

I generally find it very difficult to wait in lines or queues.

I generally walk to places quickly.

I generally drive to places quickly.

I generally get very impatient in traffic jams.

I generally find it hard to leave things unfinished (for example, a work project).

I generally hate being late for appointments.

I generally rush to reach appointments on time.

I often feel impatient in meetings.

I often bring work home or work late.

If I want something (for example, information), I generally want it now.

SEE CHAPTER 3

If you agree with more than five of the statements, your personality probably contains at least some elements of 'Type A', and this can be a source of stress in itself. 'Type A' people are continually rushing about trying to get everything done, always want everything to be perfect, and get impatient when things go wrong. They are thought to be more at risk from stress-related illnesses such as coronary heart disease and hypertension. **[Source: Friedman and Rosenman, 1974]**

'Type Bs', however, are more relaxed about everything and are likely to have lower blood pressure and less adrenaline in their blood.

Of course, most people are not either 'Type A' or 'Type B' but will be rather more one than the other, or contain elements of both types. If you find that your own approach to things is a problem, follow the three-step plan below to become less 'Type A'.

Step 1: Delight in delay

Reduce your impatience while waiting by taking something with you to read, or by treating the delay as valuable 'thinking time'. Most of us are too busy to really spend time thinking, so regard every wait as a great opportunity to be creative. Think about problems that need solving, a hobby you would like to do, or just daydream and imagine what would happen if you won the lottery or how, if you owned it, you would run the supermarket in which you are queuing.

In the car play music, or even better language or book tapes. All your waiting time will subsequently be magically transformed from an irritant into a great opportunity.

Step 2: Slow down
Make a deliberate attempt not to rush. Every time you find yourself walking very quickly, driving fast, or rushing your food, run through a short test.

1. Stop.

2. Ask yourself what will happen if you slow down. Would it be disastrous, or would the effect be inconsequential?

3. If the answer is 'inconsequential', force yourself to slow down.

Step 3: What if...?
Play the 'What if I do/What if I don't...?' game, starting with 'What if I don't... ?', and answering each of your own questions. This should help you to put things – and your life – into perspective.

What if I don't...?
What will happen if I don't finish this report today? **It will get finished tomorrow.**
What will happen if I don't get voted salesperson of the month? **I might next month.**
What will happen if I don't get to my meeting on time? **They will either wait or start without me.**

What if I do...?
What will happen if I do finish this report today? **I will be so stressed that it might affect my health.**
What will happen if I do get voted salesperson of the month? **I will probably be too tired to care.**
What will happen if I try to get to my meeting on time? **I might drive too fast and have an accident.**

And Finally...

You can find out if the strategies for stress reduction shown here are working by completing another 'stress test' after two months. Your score will hopefully reflect a much less stressed individual.

Chapter Checkpoint

After reading this chapter, you should:

- understand what stress is, and what it can do to your health.
- be aware of your own stress levels.
- have identified the cause of your stress.
- learned different strategies for dealing with stress.
- know how to deal with emotions at work.
- understand the relevance of personality to stress.

In the Next Chapter

How to assert yourself at work.

Further Reading

Sapolsky, R. M., *Why Zebras Don't Get Ulcers: A Guide to Stress and Stress-Related Disease* (New York: Freeman, 1994).

Cooper, C. L., *The Stress Check: Coping with the Stresses of Life and Work* (New Jersey: Prentice Hall, 1981).

Fontana, D., *Managing Stress* (London: BPS and Routledge, 1989).

Chandra, P., *The Complete Guide to Stress Management* (London: Optima, 1996).

Cooper, C. L., R. D. Cooper, and **L. H. Faker,** *Living with Stress* (Harmondsworth: Penguin, 1988).

Lovelace, R. T., *Stressmaster* (New York: Wiley, 1990).

Cartright, S., and **C. L. Cooper,** *No Hassle! Taking the Stress Out of Work* (London: Century Business, 1994).

Woodham, A., *Beating Stress at Work* (London: Health Education Authority, 1995).

Chapter Eight

Fight for Your Rights: Learning to be Assertive at Work

The Aim

Career advancement – respect yourself, assert yourself, advance yourself.

Many people believe that to get on at work, especially in a new job, it is necessary to acquiesce with everything that you are asked to do.

Wrong.

Making a good impression does not involve agreeing to everything. Being assertive (without being aggressive) makes a far more positive impact than simply being passive. Passivity will result in:

- an inability to say 'no'. You will take on too much, ending up either very stressed or unable to fulfil your obligations – or both.

- becoming a dogsbody, as people off-load unpopular tasks on to you.

- the feeling of being put-upon and unappreciated.

- an inability to stand up for yourself if you are treated badly by a customer, colleague or boss.

Learning to be assertive will earn you more respect, fairer treatment and reduce your stress levels as you say 'no' to inappropriate requests. You will be able to ask for things such as pay-rises; make requests; give and accept compliments; and, ultimately, progress up the career ladder.

The first step is to take an assertiveness test and also to look at your self-esteem. If you are not assertive, chances are your self-esteem will be low as well – learning to like yourself will help you to become more self-confident.

The next step is to discover the difference between assertion, aggression and passivity, and to understand exactly what assertiveness is and isn't. Having done that you can begin to take action to become more assertive, and to respect yourself as an individual. You should firstly know your rights, and understand what you are and are not entitled to ask for from others. Establishing your rights will boost your self-esteem, and will prepare you for the next stage: becoming more assertive at work. A series of strategies will guide you towards knowing what to say and do, when to say and do it, and how not to be put-upon ever again.

Finally, you will be advised how to put your new-found assertiveness skills to the test with a guide to asking your boss for a pay-rise or promotion.

1. Know Yourself

Do You Assert Yourself?

The following test will tell you whether you need to improve your assertion skills. It also establishes a baseline assessment with which you can compare yourself after the course. Make a note of your score reflecting the ease or difficulty with which you could perform each task, according to the following scheme:

1: Yes, easily.

2: Yes, but with some difficulty.

3: With great difficulty, possibly not.

4: No, probably not.

5: No, never.

If someone asked to borrow my car, a book, or a piece of gardening equipment, I could easily turn them down (if I wanted to).

I can ask someone to do me a small favour at work, such as covering for me when I am on leave, or giving me a lift somewhere.

I can usually resist sales pressure (for example, from shop assistants).

I can turn down a request for a work meeting or appointment if I don't think it is a good use of my time.

I can turn down a request for a date that I don't want.

I can tell a close colleague that something they do bothers me.

I can tell my partner or close friend that something they do bothers me.

I can ask for a pay-rise or a promotion.

If I don't know something at work, I can admit to it.

If someone asks to borrow money I can say 'no'.

If someone asks me a personal question that I don't want to answer, I can find a way to withhold the information.

I can interrupt a talkative customer or friend.

I can ask for constructive criticism.

I can request a work meeting or appointment.

If I have my request for something turned down, I can ask for an explanation.

I can tell someone if they have offended or upset me.

I can complain if I get poor service in a restaurant.

I can return defective items to a store.

I can express opinions that differ from those of the people around me.

I can tell my boss if I feel they have treated me unfairly.

I can tell my boss about a success I have had or something I have achieved.

I can resist pressure to drink.

I can request the return of borrowed items or loans.

I can receive compliments without being embarrassed.

I can ask a stranger who is annoying me in a public place to stop.

Less than 26

Your assertiveness skills seem to be fairly well-developed – you know what you want, and how to ask for it. If you would prefer, go straight to the next chapter. If, however, you want to know more about assertion, read on.

Between 26 and 60

You probably need to improve your assertion skills in at least some areas and you would be wise to read the rest of this chapter.

Between 60 and 100

You could really do with learning to be more assertive at work and in your personal life: the rest of this chapter will show you how.

Do You Like Yourself?

Consider the following statements:

I often use negative labels such as 'stupid', 'thick' or 'fat' to describe myself.

I find it difficult to accept compliments and tend to dismiss them by saying things like, "Oh, it's nothing"; "This old dress?"; or, "Anyone could have done that".

I am quick to take responsibility when things go wrong, saying things like, "It's all my fault".

I am slow to accept responsibility when things go well, saying things like, "Such and such helped me", or, "I only did this and that".

I don't like asking for help, because I don't like bothering people.

I often look back on things with regret, saying, "I should have", or, "If only I'd..."

I usually let other people have their way.

If anyone asks me what I would like to do, I respond with, "Whatever you want".

I think other peoples' happiness is more important than mine.

I often assume that other people are thinking negative thoughts about me such as, "They're so incompetent/ugly/slow".

If your answer is 'yes' to five or more of these questions it is quite possible you are suffering from low self-esteem and this is probably the partial cause of your inability to assert yourself.

The key to assertion is self-esteem. While raising your levels of assertiveness, this chapter will simultaneously aim to help you boost your self-esteem.

2. Assertion – What It Is, What It Isn't

What It Is

Assertion means standing up for your rights and acknowledging the rights of others. Assertive people do not allow others to take advantage of them, nor do they take advantage of other people. They know their rights as human beings, and they have enough self-esteem to take action when those rights are being violated.

Being assertive involves:

- knowing what you want.

- knowing whether what you want is fair and reasonable.

- knowing that what you want does not violate anyone else's rights.

- asking for what you want (if it is fair and does not violate other peoples' rights).

- not being afraid to take risks.

- being calm and relaxed in your actions.

- expressing your feelings openly.

- being able to say 'no' when appropriate, without feeling guilty.

- giving and taking compliments easily.

- giving and taking fair criticism.

- coping with unfair criticism without it affecting your self-esteem.

What It Isn't

Michael works in publishing and has a problem with one of his colleagues, Anthony. Anthony is frequently late for meetings, and asks Michael to cover for him. He is also fairly unreliable, depending on Michael to jump in at the last minute to rescue projects or tasks that he has been unable to complete. Michael has put up with this behaviour from Anthony for well over a year and the result is that Michael has ended up doing half Anthony's job as well as his own. To make matters worse, Anthony claims credit for the work that Michael has finished off for him.

Michael decided one day to tackle Anthony. His first attempt was a bit of a failure. He went up to Anthony's desk and said, "Anthony, I don't suppose you have a minute? I mean, I know how busy you are trying to finish the report but, if you can spare a minute, I'd like to talk to you."

Unfortunately, Anthony waved him away, muttering something about being "Up to my eyes in it."

Michael sighed and scuttled off.

He next broached the subject over coffee, and this time he was able to say what he wanted. The conversation went like this:

"Anthony, look, I hope you don't mind me mentioning this. I know this has been going on for a very long time – and I'm sure that there might be good reason for it – but is there any possible way that you could possibly try not to leave me your work at the last moment – I'm sure you don't mean any harm, and I'm happy to help out... more than happy... but I am getting stressed over all the extra work I have to do."

"No problem," Anthony replied, and changed the subject.

Michael felt good. He had made his request, and the expected row or argument hadn't materialised. Michael had even been worried that Anthony would fall out with him and end their friendship. He felt very relieved.

However, over the next few weeks, it seemed as if the conversation had never happened. Anthony's behaviour changed for a day or so, but quickly slipped back into the old patterns.

This time, Michael was flummoxed. He also began to feel a little angry, which was most unlike him. But he didn't know what to do – after all, speaking to Anthony hadn't worked, had it?

Things came to a head one day when Anthony dumped a project on Michael because he had a 'hot date'. Michael had an important engagement that evening too, and he finally snapped. He started to shout:

"Stop keep taking advantage of me and do your own work for a change. You're just selfish and lazy!"

Anthony was extremely taken aback. He had never seen this side to Michael and couldn't really understand where it had come from. After all, Michael had always been happy to help out before. Sure, he had once muttered something about Anthony not leaving things to give Michael to the last minute, but that was only a temporary complaint, wasn't it? Anthony took his work and resolved never to ask Michael for any help in the future. He also hardly spoke to Michael anymore and relationships between them became very strained.

Passivity

At first Michael was passive. Passivity involves failing to stand up for your rights, expressing your needs diffidently or apologetically, or being unable to express them honestly.

Passive responses are made with the aims of avoiding conflict and pleasing others with an underlying message of 'You are more important than me, and I'm wrong'.

The passive or non-assertive person probably believes that if they do stand up for their rights or express an opinion then others will be angry or incredulous. Alternatively, the passive individual thinks that they have no rights, or that their opinions are wrong or unimportant.

People often confuse passivity with polite or helpful behaviour. Admittedly it minimises confrontation, but amongst its disadvantages is the fact that self-esteem will be dramatically lowered.

Aggression

After being passive Michael switched to aggression in an attempt to stand up for his rights.

Unlike assertion, which acknowledges that everybody has rights, aggression is based on the belief that only you have rights or needs. Aggressive people certainly stand up for themselves, but usually at the expense of others' feelings or rights.

Such individuals usually get their way – because people are frightened of them or want to get rid of them. They are unlikely, however, to be popular or to advance in the workplace, as they are often seen simply as the office bully.

Aggression, passivity, assertion

The following table illustrates some common non-verbal and verbal examples of aggressive, passive and assertive behaviour.

Aggressive behaviour	Passive behaviour	Assertive behaviour
Shouting/loud voice.	Quiet, small, hesitant voice.	Calm, controlled voice.
Pointing finger.	Clenched, wringing hands; hands smoothing clothes; or fluttering hands.	Hands still, or one hand in pocket.
Phrases such as: "You'd better..."	Phrases such as: "I think..."	Phrases such as: "Maybe..."
Glaring eyes.	Downcast eyes.	Direct eye contact, glancing away at times to avoid glaring.
Hands on hips.	Hands clenched, or one hand gripping arm tightly.	Hands by side.
Rigid posture.	Stooped posture.	Upright, but relaxed posture.
Philosophy: 'I don't care about you'.	Philosophy: 'I don't care about me'.	Philosophy: 'I care about me and you'.
Saying: "I want you to do this!" or, "What are you talking about?"	Saying: "Would you mind very much if...?" or, "I'm not sure if I agree..."	Saying: "I would like..." or, "How can we resolve this?"

Michael let Anthony take advantage of him, sending the message that Anthony's rights were more important than his own. When he confronted Anthony the first time, he dressed his request up in so many qualifications and asked it so passively that Anthony did not take it seriously. His final confrontation, however, was aggressive and accused Anthony of things that he was not even aware of.

The first thing Michael should have done was to examine his own self-esteem. By letting Anthony off-load work on to him it was clear that Michael did not think he or his time was as important as that of his colleague.

Michael had a self-esteem problem.

3. Your Self-esteem

Self-esteem is an important part of assertiveness. You can't very well stand up for your rights or express your opinions if you don't feel you deserve any rights or that your opinions are invariably wrong.

Research shows that people with low self-esteem do not believe themselves to be equal to others and cannot find cause to object to being badly treated. [Source: Davis Robbins and McKay, 1995]

How to Boost Your Self-Esteem

You will only consider yourself equal if you like yourself, and you can only like yourself if you don't judge yourself negatively.

See the positive bits
Make a list of the positive aspects to your personality. Are you kind, gentle generous, friendly and so on? Ask a friend to help you; be honest and not too modest.

See the achievements
Make another list of the things that you have achieved in your life or that you are proud of. These could be things from school or from later in life – they do not need to be major events. For example, you might be proud of having helped a friend, gained a degree or had a child.

Remind yourself
Whenever your self-esteem needs a boost, review these lists to remind yourself of why you should feel good about yourself.

All this is extremely important in the quest to boost your self-esteem and thus improve your assertion skills. Ultimately, however, your ability to raise your levels of both self-esteem and subsequently of assertiveness hang on your awareness of one vital concept – that of rights.

4. Your Rights

Also of fundamental importance when seeking to increase levels of assertiveness and self-esteem are rights.

Children are often wrongly taught that:

- it's selfish to put your own needs first.

- it's rude to ask for what you want – better to wait and see what you are given.

- your opinions are not as valuable as those of adults.

- you cannot possibly make decisions all by yourself.

- you should always try and help others, at whatever cost to yourself.

- mistakes are to be avoided.

- changing your mind is weak.

- you should always say 'yes' if someone wants to be with you – it's rude to say 'no'.

Whatever you learnt as a child, remember that you have:

- the right to put yourself first sometimes.

- the right to ask for what you want – while realising that the other person has the right to say 'no'.

- the right to have opinions, convictions, feelings and emotions, and to express them appropriately.

- the right to make your own decisions and to cope with the consequences.
- the right to choose whether or not to get involved with the problems of someone else.
- the right to make mistakes.
- the right to change your mind or to decide on a different course of action.
- the right to privacy.
- the right to be happy.
- the right to be treated fairly by others.
- the right to make choices.
- the right to be fully briefed and well-informed.
- the right not to act on the advice of others.
- the right to say 'no'.
- the right to be treated with respect.
- the right to change yourself and to become assertive.

Note – you have no right to:

- expect or insist that others give you what you want.
- get involved in someone else's problems if they don't want you involved.
- expect others to be infallible.
- insist that others never change their minds.
- invade the privacy of other people.
- be happy at the expense of other people's happiness.
- expect others not to change.
- make choices for other people.
- withhold information from others without good reason.
- expect others always to say 'yes'.
- be disrespectful of others.

5. How to Become More Assertive

Step 1: Speaking
Non-assertive people speak in non-assertive ways. The main problem is not what they say, but how they say it.

- Communicate directly. Decide what you want to say and say it without unnecessary qualification or elaboration.

- Stick to the point. If you are making a request, don't be side-tracked. Know what you want and don't come away before your request has been considered.

- Use the broken record technique, a method which avoids giving in to something you can't or don't want to do; simply repeating your request or refusal until the other person accepts it – like a broken record. At the same time, listen to and acknowledge what the other person is saying.

  Example:
  Boss: *"Could you stay late and help me with a paper I need to prepare?"*
  You: *"I'm sorry. I would normally, but I have another arrangement for tonight."*
  Boss: *"But I need to get this done!"*
  You: *"I'm sorry, I've already made important plans for tonight."*
  Boss: *"But I said it would be done for tomorrow!"*
  You: *"Yes, but I'm afraid I can't stay late tonight."*

- Learn to say 'no' – without apologising profusely. Always remember that it is within your rights to say 'no'; a simple "Sorry, but…" should suffice.

  Example:
  Colleague: *"Could we meet for an hour this afternoon to discuss the new proposal?"*
  Wrong Answer: *"I'm sorry, but unfortunately I have other plans this afternoon. I'm really sorry about this, but I made these plans ages ago and I just can't change them – I'm so sorry and I hope it doesn't inconvenience you."*
  Right Answer: *"I'm sorry, but I have other plans this afternoon which I just can't change."*

- Delay – assertively. If someone makes a request that you do not wish to accept, but have no good reason to refuse, try a simple delaying tactic.

  Example:
  "Can I get back to you on that one?"
  or:
  "OK, let me think about that."
  or:
  "I need to check my schedule."

- Reflection. Use this technique when you are asked to do something you do not want to or cannot do. It involves reflecting back that you understand what the other person is asking, and that you know how they feel.

  Example:
  Boss: *"I really need you to help me tonight."*
  You: *"I know that you need to get the paper written tonight, but I can't stay late."*

- Use a raincheck refusal. In other words, say 'no', but agree to the request some other time.

Step 2: Speaking without words

If you look apologetic, uncomfortable or embarrassed, then what you say is irrelevant – you will still come across as unassertive.

If, on the other hand, you look confident and self-assured, you will create the impression of being confident and self-assured. People will take notice of you and of what you are saying.

- Maintain eye contact. Look the other person in the eye – avoid looking away, looking at the floor, or glancing round nervously.

- Stand straight and upright. Avoid slouching or trying to make yourself appear smaller. Push your shoulders back, reach your full height and face the other person square on.

- Speak in a firm and steady voice. Don't shout or whisper.

- Keep your hands firmly by your side – don't fidget with things on your desk, or in your pocket.

Step 3: Catching thoughts

What we think affects how we act and behave on a profound level. Passive people can become more assertive by identifying their non-assertive thoughts and replacing them with new ones. It isn't easy but it is worth the effort.

False thoughts

Some of the thoughts passive people with low self-esteem have are simply false and should be replaced with more assertive ideas.

> **Example:**
> *"My opinion doesn't count."*
> *"If I speak up, people won't like me."*
> *"I am not as important as the others are."*

Irrational thoughts

Other thoughts may not be false, but they are irrational.

For instance, some people find it hard to be assertive because they want everybody to like them. Admittedly being assertive sometimes means that those who have been taking advantage of you will indeed like you less, but that should not be a problem. It is impossible for everyone to like you and if that is your goal, you will never be able to live life according to your own values and desires.

Another common irrational belief for many people is that they must have the approval of other people. Certainly, having the approval of others is nice, but there will be times when it is necessary to accept that someone else disapproves. Time spent trying to gain others' approval unnecessarily is time wasted rather than being used for more fruitful and important activities.

The Diary Technique
Learn to 'catch' your thoughts by keeping a diary. In it, you should write down any thoughts associated with a situation in which you found it difficult to be assertive. Write next to them more positive, replacement thoughts.

Situation	Negative Thoughts	Positive Ones
I want to ask for a pay-rise.	My boss will say 'no'. They will think me arrogant for asking. They will point out why I don't deserve it. I will feel bad.	They may say 'no' – but they may say 'yes'. They will admire me for asking; it shows I believe in myself. I will point out why I deserve it. I will not feel bad if rejected, I will be proud that I tried.
I want to ask my office-partner to spend less time chatting on the phone while I am trying to work.	They will be offended. They will be angry. We will fall out.	If I do it in a sensitive way they will not be offended. They will only be angry if I do it aggressively. We won't fall out because at the same time I will praise some other aspect of their behaviour.

Step 4: Giving – and receiving – compliments
Many people feel awkward about giving and receiving compliments but assertiveness includes expressing positive feelings and ideas, as well as negative ones.

Receiving
Those people who are not very assertive or who have low self-esteem often have difficulty accepting compliments.

Example:
Person A: *"I like your shirt – the colour really suits you."*
Person B: *"Oh, this old thing – I've had it for ages!"*

Person A: *"You did a really good job on that marketing presentation."*
Person B: *"Oh, it wasn't me – I got a lot of help."*

Part of becoming assertive is learning to accept compliments from other people in an assertive and graceful manner. Compliments should not be dismissed, but accepted with a smile and a 'thank you'. If you really disagree with the compliment you can put your own view across anyway – but remember that the other person still has the right to think you're great!

In short, accept, acknowledge and agree with the compliment.

Example:
Person A: *"I like your shirt – the colour really suits you."*
Person B: *"Thanks – it's one of my favourites."*
Person A: *"You did a really good job on that marketing presentation."*
Person B: *"Thanks very much. I put a lot of effort into it."*

Giving

Having learned to accept compliments and having become aware of how good they are for you, you should start giving them – where appropriate, of course. Speak in a firm, confident voice, preferably looking directly at the other person.

You will find that if you are able to compliment people, it will be easier to make complaints about them; your complaints will appear not to be random and unjustified, but necessary, and will be better accepted if people know that you are usually complimentary.

Step 5: Taking responsibility

Recognise your own role

Being assertive also involves taking responsibility for your life and for choices in your life. This means making your own decisions, not simply drifting, or going along with other peoples' choices.

It also means not blaming people or circumstances for what happens. If you take responsibility for your own life, you can change any parts you don't like. If you blame outside circumstances for what happens to you, it implies a helplessness and an inability to change anything.

> Psychologists refer to people who take personal responsibility for their actions as having 'internal locus of control', while those who feel that external events or people are responsible for what happens to them are said to have 'external locus of control'. [Source: Rotter, 1966]

Recognise your limits

However, you should remember that there are certain things for which you cannot be held responsible, including:

- other people's actions.

- other people's decisions.

- other people's happiness.

You are responsible for any direct consequences of your actions but not for the reactions of others to those consequences. For example, if you criticise a colleague, you are responsible for the possibility that you may hurt their feelings but you are not responsible for the way they react to your criticism. In other words, if they threaten to resign or leave their job this is not your responsibility.

Own your language

One of the best ways to take responsibility for your life is to acknowledge ownership of your feelings, opinions and ideas. This is best achieved by accepting ownership and responsibility in your choice of words.

Take ownership in your language, and in your life, by:

- being specific. Say, in other words, "I don't know if I can meet this deadline", rather than, "You give me too much work to do".

- stressing the 'I'. Say, for example, "I want to do this"; or, "I believe this".

  Example:

  "I'm feeling really stressed."

  Here the speaker is acknowledging that the stress is their responsibility, and theirs to handle and reduce.

  "It's really stressful here."

  The speaker here is relinquishing responsibility and blaming the environment for their feelings of stress, and is thus unlikely to be able – or to choose – to reduce it.

- using simple language. Too many people qualify statements by adding adjectives or offering so much explanation that ultimately the listener doesn't know what they are trying to communicate.

- being honest. It is your right to feel the way you do, and your feelings are valid.

Step 6: Complaining assertively

There is an important difference between complaints and criticisms. Complaints are justified comments about something that may be impinging on your rights. They are constructive – their aim is not to hurt, but to assertively explain what the problem is. Unlike complaints, criticisms are put-downs which are intended to hurt.

Making a complaint

Firstly, think carefully about your motives. Do you want to put someone down (criticism) or do you want to give them straightforward, honest feedback which may help them and you?

Once you have decided that it is a complaint you wish to make, follow the guidelines below to ensure that it is made in an effective and assertive manner.

- Be specific. It is more useful to say:

  "You left the photocopier without paper again."
  than to say:
  "You always use up supplies without replacing them."

- Acknowledge the positive. If you can include some genuinely positive comment, do so. Say, for example:

  "It's great sharing an office with you – I've learnt so much. I get a bit worried, though, when you leave the door open. Could you lock it when you leave?"

- Keep calm. Keep your voice level, and avoid getting angry or abusive.

- Keep to the point. Don't let other complaints cloud the issue, and don't allow yourself to get side-tracked. Remember the broken record technique.

- Focus on behaviour alone. Don't attack the whole person, only the aspect of their behaviour which is troubling you. Say, for example:

  "It's frustrating for me when you say you will take on a piece of work but then don't have time to complete it."
  not:
  "You're so unreliable!"

- Avoid labels or stereotypes like, "You're such a typical accountant!"

- Be constructive. If appropriate, make a constructive suggestion as to how the person could change their behaviour. For example, don't say,

  "For heavens sake, can't you be more punctual?"
  say instead:
  "Could you remember that when you're early for a meeting it helps the rest of us present an organised front?"

- Take responsibility for your complaint. For example, say:

  "I get frustrated if I have to back you up in meetings when you have not prepared your material."
  not:
  "Why don't you ever come prepared to meetings?"

> **Golden Rule**
> When complaining to others, be as specific as you can about your complaint, and avoid generalisations.

Step 7: Accepting a complaint or criticism assertively

Criticism or complaints about yourself may be useful or useless, valid or invalid, reasonable or unreasonable. It is up to you to decide how much notice you want to take. Inevitably critical comments will be taken personally, and even with unfounded criticism the recipient feels hurt. Three different techniques can be used for dealing with criticism.

Agreement

Calmly agree with any complaints that are true or fair. Acknowledge the point being made and apologise (but don't over-apologise or put yourself down). If possible, offer a brief explanation, or try to add a positive statement about what you will do to improve the situation.

Example:
Your boss: *"That presentation was really lousy."*
You: *"Yes, you're right, it could have been better. I had technical problems last week. But that's all sorted now, so the next one should be fine."*

Probing

How do you know if the other person is giving you constructive feedback or simply being nasty? The 'probing' technique will help you to decide if your critic is making a helpful comment, or merely wants to put you down.

Ask the critic to explain or expand on the comment. If they are just trying to put you down they will often be reluctant, or unable, to expand. If they are genuinely trying to be helpful, their expansion could be very valuable – you may learn something.

Example:

Critic: *"It's clear from your presentation that speaking in public isn't really your strong point, is it?"*
You: *"Really? What was it that I did that made you think that?"*
Put-down: *"Oh, just generally – you could just tell."*
Genuine: *"Well, you did seem very nervous and fidgety – maybe you should practice speaking in public a bit; I'll give you a hand."*

Partial agreement

This will help you to cope with manipulative criticism designed expressly to put you down. There may be an element of truth in what is being said, but the critic has probably exaggerated the situation.

The technique of partial agreement is to calmly acknowledge that there may be some fairness in what is being said. The aim is to stop the criticism and thus protect your self-esteem.

Example:

Your boss: *"Your sales figures have been terrible this month. You haven't achieved anywhere near the average – probably because you've been late so often, and when you have been here, your mind has clearly been elsewhere..."*
You: *"Yes, you're right, my figures are down."*

Step 8: Requests: making them, refusing them

Making them

Requests are easy to make if you think well of yourself. If not, even the most reasonable request can be difficult, and if it is refused you feel rejected, thinking perhaps that, 'I am not worth it or entitled to it'. Nobody is confident about everything, but assertion will give you the opportunity to get what you want. Regardless of whether or not you succeed your self-esteem can only be increased by trying.

Incidentally, timing is also crucial when making a request. Read your boss's mood appropriately – if they are particularly short-tempered and harassed, it might not be a good time. Alternatively, make a point of staging your request at a fortuitous moment for you – when you've been praised, for example.

Firstly, fears of what will happen if the request is refused must be overcome.

- **They might say 'no'.** Yes, they might – it is within the other person's right to refuse your request. It doesn't reflect on you personally. You didn't obtain what you asked for but asking assertively for what you want is a success in itself.

- **I will feel rejected.** If you see the 'no' as a personal affront then yes, you will feel rejected. If, however, you see it as a simple exercising of the other person's rights, you shouldn't feel rejected. They have not rejected you – only your request.

- **They'll dislike me.** Why should they think badly of you? If they don't want to help you, they can always turn you down. The whole point of being assertive is to recognise your right to make requests – and the other person's right to turn them down.

Refusing them

Turning down requests is often much harder than making them – many people find it very difficult to say 'no'.

Why it's hard to say 'no'	How to overcome this
The other person may feel hurt or rejected.	Remember – you're not responsible for how people react to your (reasonable) decisions.
They may not like me anymore.	If this is the case, then they are not respecting your right to say 'no' – you're better off without them.
They might never ask me again.	You can only deal with the current situation. You could add that you might be willing to say 'yes' another time.
I want to please them.	You shouldn't want to please others at your own expense. Take another look at your self-esteem.

How to say 'no'

Say it clearly and firmly, without over-qualification. Give a reason if necessary, but only if it is genuine. Just providing an excuse may give the other person a chance to find a way round your refusal.

Don't give the other person an opportunity to talk you out of your refusal – politely change the subject or leave the room.

6. Asking for a Pay-Rise or Promotion

One of the requests that people have most difficulty in making is to ask for a pay-rise or promotion. Modesty – often misplaced – means that people frequently don't feel able to actively promote their talents.

Someone who – for the right reasons – asks for a pay-rise is someone who recognises their own worth. Most managers and bosses are impressed by workers who have confidence in their abilities. Thus the act of asking for a pay-rise – even if you don't get it – can create a favourable impression.

Do You Deserve It?

Before approaching your boss ask yourself if you deserve your pay-rise/promotion. Your reasons should be genuine, and should not include the following:

- the fact that you have been in the company any length of time. Longevity does not warrant automatic pay-rises or promotions.

- the fact that a colleague has had a rise or promotion. This is totally irrelevant.

- the fact that someone in a rival company is earning more than you.

Genuine reasons for deserving a pay-rise must be positive, and connected with what you have achieved. Good reasons include the following:

- the fact that, for example, you sold more products than anyone else this year.

- the fact that you had an idea which saved the company £20,000 last year.

- the fact that you have achieved things above and beyond your job description.

- the fact that you have been offered a job elsewhere which offers more money (only to be used if this is absolutely true).

How to Ask

Ask for a meeting with your boss. Don't just turn up unannounced or have a chat in the corridor. In the meeting, get straight to the point by stating in a clear and calm voice, "I am here to discuss promotion/a pay-rise". Present the evidence to support your case. Don't be aggressive or defensive, just calmly state your reasons.

Don't be tempted to talk in the silence that may follow. Sit back confidently (but not arrogantly), and allow your boss to consider what you have just said. Answer your boss's questions, comments or criticisms assertively, using the techniques outlined previously in this chapter.

What If... How to Cope with All Possible Scenarios

What if...?	Respond with...
Your boss won't listen to you and says 'no'.	"I appreciate your answer, but I'd still like the opportunity to explain why I deserve a rise. I understand what you say about there being no money at the moment, but an agreement from you that in principle I deserve the rise would be reassuring."
Your boss disagrees that you deserve the rise.	Listen to what they say and decide whether they have a valid point. Don't feel discouraged – they may be giving you valuable feedback. If they are being unreasonable, you may have to accept the inevitable and start looking for promotion elsewhere. **Remember:** if you hadn't asked for promotion, you wouldn't know where you stood.
Your boss agrees that you are deserving, but says that they can't give you a rise because 'everyone will expect one'.	"I am here on my own behalf. I never discuss my pay with anyone else, so if someone approaches you, they'll be doing so independently of me."

Chapter Checkpoint

After reading this chapter, you should:

- have established how assertive you are, and what level of self-esteem you have.
- know what assertion is and how it differs from aggression and passivity.
- have learnt how to boost your self-esteem.
- know what your rights are.
- know what steps to take to become more assertive.
- have the confidence to ask for a pay-rise or promotion.

In the Next Chapter

How to climb the career ladder.

Further Reading

Mansfield, P., *Why Am I Afraid to be Assertive?* (London: Fount, 1994).

Lindenfield, G., *Assert Yourself: A Self-Help Assertiveness Programme for Men and Women* (London: Thorsons, 1992).

Back, K., *Assertiveness At Work: A Practical Guide to Handling Awkward Situations* (Maidenhead: McGraw-Hill, 1991).

Chapter Nine

Onwards and Upwards: Climbing the Career Ladder

The Aim
Career advancement.

If you have been following the advice in this book it is probable that you will find yourself immensely employable and promotable. Having reached this stage there are further, more advanced skills that you will need to progress, and techniques that will provide valuable ammunition when promotion opportunities arise.

The first skill a worker should be aware of is that of planning a career. Some people choose a career path very early on, and subsequently regret it; others drift from job to job; yet more have the right career, but don't know how to plan ahead. Career planning is, therefore, a vital skill.

Having done that, one of the secrets in managing a career involves coping with, and benefiting from, change. Workers must be able to adapt easily, as they face the new technologies, new working patterns, new organisational structures, and new co-workers that may be introduced by organisations in their efforts to become ever more competitive. Furthermore, as you progress, not only will you have to manage your own reaction to change, but also that of other people such as your subordinates.

With subordinates in mind, of course, one of the first signs of career progression occurs when you start to become responsible for other employees. You may become a manager or supervisor, or you may simply be an unofficial leader within a work group. Since it is difficult to be promoted too far in many job roles without taking on leadership responsibilities, those who can demonstrate good leadership potential are likely to progress more quickly up the career path.

1. Planning

Career planning begins with a clear understanding of what a career is, as opposed to a job.

A job is something we do in order to earn money to live. A career is a pattern or programme of related work experiences spanning the individual's working life. Or, as one source puts it, a career is 'the sequence of employment-related positions, roles, activities and experiences encountered by a person'. [Source: Arnold, Cooper and Robertson, 1998]

Why Plan?

A changing world

The changing scene of employment and developments in the labour market have major implications for career-planning. The structures of organisations are altering: layers of management are being eliminated (delayering) and less people are being employed (downsizing).

Increased global competition means that companies in the West need to reduce costs in order to compete. There is an increasing trend towards short-term contracts and greater self-employment or varying working patterns. All these changes result in workers needing to look ahead and to keep updating their skills and knowledge in order to remain eminently employable.

Early choices are not always the best choices

Many people drift into jobs on the basis of choices they made when they were teenagers. They chose science GCSEs or A Levels, and so became lab technicians. They chose to study accountancy at university, so their career was mapped out by the age of 17. For some people this works very well – but for others, such early choices are not always the best in the long term, for some of the following reasons:

- people find themselves bored of the career they chose as a teenager.

- they realise that they are in their parents' chosen profession, not theirs.

- they find themselves out of a job or in a precarious industry.

- they discover other options that they did not know existed before.

Help! I'm in the Wrong Job

Daniel was 30 years old, and had been working as a biomedical technician for 7 years when he started contemplating a career change. He said:

"I'm bored of working in a lab. I want to work with people, not slides and samples. But I don't know what I can do. I've got no other training or experiences. How can I afford to re-train? What will I re-train as?"

As Daniel realised, it is possible to spend your entire life in a job that you don't enjoy, simply because you have no idea of what you are best at. Don't be one of these people. The following three-step plan gives guidelines to follow for anyone who is unsure about what direction to take.

Step 1: Assess yourself

Consult a professional

Finding out where your skills lie and what qualities you have is not easy, and it is probably best to consult a professional careers counsellor. Such a person can probably be found locally; alternatively, if you are a graduate, your university careers centre may provide you with such a service.

Some careers counsellors prefer to use in-depth interviews rather than pen-and-paper tests, and these can be just as effective, if not more so.

Take a test

The advisor will probably ask you to sit a test to assess what your skills are and how they could best be put to use.

The best tests are those that ask you a hundred or so questions designed to tease out your skills and personal characteristics, and subsequently present you with a selection of careers that would best suit you.

The researcher J. Holland developed a theory of vocational education and planning that stresses the match between the characteristics of the person and those of the work environment.

Holland's theory assumes that most people can be classified into six general types which reflect a general orientation towards a certain career.

Type	Personal Characteristics	Sample Occupations
Realistic.	Shy, genuine, materialistic, persistent.	Mechanical engineer, waiter.
Investigative.	Analytical, cautious, curious, independent, introverted.	Economist, scientist.
Artistic.	Disordered, emotional, idealistic imaginative, impulsive.	Journalist, actor, copywriter.
Social.	Co-operative, sociable, generous.	Teacher, counsellor, social worker
Enterprising.	Adventurous, ambitious, confident.	Entrepreneur, personnel manager, lawyer.
Conventional.	Efficient, obedient, practical, conscientious.	Typist, secretary, lab technician.

[Source: Holland, 1985]

A typical test assesses participants on the following traits:

- decision-making ability.
- leadership potential.
- initiative.
- team player ability.
- verbal communication skill.
- written communication skill.
- extroversion/introversion traits.
- problem-solving skills.

- planning skills.

- risk-taking ability.

- sensitivity.

- stress tolerance.

- perseverance.

Step 2: Do some research
Once you have an idea of what career would suit you, the next stage is to engage in some research.

Daniel, a graduate, completed a computerised assessment at his old university careers centre and it came up with a list of ten possible professions, all emphasising a 'people' element, from police officer to psychologist. He was able to discount five on the basis that the training required was too long or too expensive, or because the job held no appeal. He finally decided on the possibility of re-training as a physiotherapist. This would match his science background and would enable him to stay in the medical field, while working with people. The only snag was that it required three years of re-training, leading Daniel to Step 3.

Step 3: Plan a strategy
Once Daniel knew what he wanted he began a long-term strategy to help him achieve his goal. He decided to move back in with his parents to save money until the new academic year started, when he would enrol on a physiotherapy training course.

Having assessed yourself, established a range of careers, and decided which one you wish to pursue, you should devise a strategy enabling you to reach your goal.

Right Job – But No Plan?
Once settled in your chosen career, you need a way of planning advancement within your profession.

Test yourself
Ask yourself the following questions:

Do I have a five-year career plan?
Am I on schedule in my plan – in other words, am I where I hoped I would be when I devised my plan?
Have I ever taken a transfer, new job or promotion just because it fits my career plan?
Have I sought new training or experiences to enable me to reach my planned goals?
Do I have a mentor or role model who guides my career?

If your answer is 'yes' to all five statements, then you would appear to have planned ahead quite adequately. If not, read on...

Step 1: Find a role-model
Meera is a secretary for a small legal firm who has her sights set on being a television press officer. She knows of someone in her local TV company in this role who started as a secretary, and identified the following qualities of this individual: confidence, experience and skill.

Identifying a role model gives you an idea of the person you want to become in ten years' time. This could be a chief executive, a top manager or someone from another company. It could even be a public figure.

Once you have identified the person, work out what skills and qualifications you would need in order to get where they are.

Step 2: Assess yourself
Develop an accurate picture of your talents, interests, skills and experiences. Most importantly, you should identify those gaps that need filling before you can make it to the top.

Meera drew up two lists, one with her skills and the other with her shortcomings:

Skills	Shortcomings
Typing Administration Organisation Communication	No experience dealing with the press. No television experience. No public relations experience.

Step 3: Define your goals
Using Steps 1 and 2 as the basis of your assessment, develop some realistic career goals.

For Meera, this meant a three-year plan to gain more experience dealing with the press and public relations, and to gain some experience in television. She implemented a strategy that involved:

- asking her manager if she could start a public relations campaign for their firm with the local media (an offer that they were delighted to accept).

- enrolling on an evening course in public relations run at her local college.

- sending a letter to her local TV station, asking if she could spend a day shadowing their press officer – they agreed.

Step 4: Frequently reassess your goals
Claire's long-term goal to become UK Customer Service Manager of an international telecommunications company was disrupted by an offer to take a well-paid position in America – in Training. She took the job and loved it so much that she changed her goal to that of becoming Training Officer of America's Mid-West region.

Giles wanted to be a partner in the legal firm he worked for, and worked long hours to achieve his goal. When his wife had their first child, his priorities changed and he decided to set up his own firm so that he could delegate more and spend more time with his child.

It is important to continually re-examine your career aims and strategies. Circumstances change, and life events that may result in a reassessment of your strategies and goals include:

- marriage and/or children.
- relocation.
- the death of a family member.
- new (and unexpected) career opportunities.

Beware – Career Pitfalls

Watch out for the following career traps.

Taking a job or promotion because the pay is good

As a student, Matthew was offered a Ph.D. studentship with a grant at a top university. He was also offered a well-paid post at a minor and little-known college. He took the paid post with the result that, five years on, he has no Ph.D. and no kudos from being at a good university. His career prospects were sacrificed for three years of salary.

Going after the money without considering other factors is, ultimately, a short-sighted goal: many people who make such a move slow down their progress along the career path.

Drifting

Many people float from job to job in the hope that one day they will find what they are looking for. They may eventually, but their progress will be hampered by a CV which tells the real story – that here is someone who does not know what they want. Each 'drift' reduces employability.

Spending only a short time in a job is a common mistake made by ambitious people. They start a job, then six months later, see a better one. Again, their CV proclaims that this person cannot stay in a job and will move on; once more, employability may be drastically reduced.

Always aim to stay for at least a year, unless the job is truly unbearable.

Leaving on bad terms

It is tempting to tell your manager what you really think of them when you leave a job. Resist the temptation: it will come back to haunt you forever in the form of a poor reference.

Always try to leave on the best terms possible. Bad references are of course undesirable, while potential employers will think it strange if you do not put your previous manager down as a referee.

If you have left on bad terms, the best way to deal with this is simply not to put your former boss down as a referee, and to come up with a plausible explanation for this: for example, they have moved, or left the country. But beware – you might get caught out if you lie. One person who was fired from his post did not put his employer down as a referee, but admitted to potential employers that he was asked to leave. He was lucky – he worked in an industry where qualified workers were in short supply and he quickly found a new job.

2. Adapting

At the beginning of the new millennium, only one thing is certain – that nothing is guaranteed. Change is inevitable as we progress and evolve, and this has never been more so than in today's organisations. The workers who are able to cope with or even manage the change process will be the ones with the edge over their more reticent colleagues. As one source puts it, 'Change is an inescapable part of both social and organisational life'. [Source: Mullins, 1996] Companies are constantly looking for new ways in which to gain a competitive edge, and may well implement new strategies, including:

- changing the management structure.

- merging with other companies.

- taking over, or being taken over by, other companies.

- introducing new product lines.

- introducing new ways of working.

- redundancies.

- creating new jobs.

- introducing new technology.

- changing attitudes towards customer service.

One study found that 51 per cent of companies surveyed were experiencing major transformations [Source: Ezzamel, Green, Lilley, and Willmott, 1994], while a survey of the Institute of Management in the UK reported that 80 per cent of its managers had experienced restructuring in their organisation within the last five years. [Source: Wheatley, 1992]

How We React to Change

"Our manager came in one day and told us that we were merging with a larger company. There was uproar as we all struggled to come to terms with what might happen. We were full of questions: what would happen to our jobs; what would happen with our offices; would we lose our systems; would we have to adopt new rules and regulations...? The manager could not answer any of our questions and we were left feeling a bit shell-shocked, really. My first reaction was to get out. I had been in

the company four years and was happy there. I had my own office, I knew the struc-
tures and the bureaucracy. I figured that if I was going to have to get used to a
whole new regime, I may as well do it in another company – at least I would be able
to see what I was getting into there. Here it was unknown."

Iain, Telecommunications Operator

"We had a new boss and he decided that he had to make his mark. He started to
change the way things were done... It was small things at first, like how we filled in
our expense claim forms. Then he started questioning our claims – asking to see
them before signing them off. He began to get very autocratic, and we were just
afraid of what he would do next. Suddenly we didn't know where we stood anymore,
or what the rules were."

Bryony, Journalist

"My company introduced electronic communication recently, and it scared the living
daylights out of me. I wasn't brought up with computers and I thought I was doing
well to learn how to use a word-processing package – in fact, it was quite good and
now I can't imagine how I ever managed without it. But email... I just can't see the
point of sending these email things when memos or faxes have done the job well for
years. Why change? I refused to, and I do miss out on some messages that only get
sent on email. But that's the sender's fault isn't it? They should send them by memo,
too."

Hamish, Accountant

"I had heard rumours for months that our work phone numbers were going to be
changed, but I never heard anything definite. One day I returned from holiday to find
that my number had changed, along with everyone else's. I was angry – I had let-
ter-heads and business cards with the old numbers. I had not told any of my clients
of the change. I lost a huge amount of business and as I work on commission, I was
furious. The only response I got from my complaints was that 'everyone was told'. I
wasn't, not officially. Being told some vague rumour on the grapevine isn't enough,
is it?"

Paula, Sales Executive

Many people resist change – indeed, as one author says, 'People are naturally wary
of change'. [Source: Mullins, 1996] Why?

We dislike change because we have a need to control and predict our environment. When we know what is happening and what will happen we feel safe and
secure. Change threatens all that. We no longer know what will happen. All our safety systems are at risk.

How You Feel About Change

The first stage to coping with and managing change is to be receptive to it, and to
expect it.

To find out how receptive to change you are make a note of the statements with
which you agree in the following assessment test.

> When I think about my organisation, I cannot imagine how it will succeed for another five years without change.
>
> I believe that changes are a necessary part of organisational development.
>
> I like new ideas and visions.
>
> I get bored doing the same thing day in, day out.
>
> When I think of changes that I have undergone in my life, or that have happened to me in this job, I realise that they generally turned out for the best.
>
> I am constantly looking for new challenges.
>
> I am often one of the first people I know to latch on to a trend, or to buy a new gadget.
>
> I don't have a regular routine each day, either at work or at home.

The more statements you agree with the more receptive you are to change. However, even for those with a high level of adaptability, the following four-step plan to managing change will provide clear guidelines for dealing with uncertainty and transformation.

The following four strategies are based on the basic premise that effective management of change must be based on a clear understanding of human behaviour in the workplace. Individuals do bring their feelings to work, and will become emotional and concerned about how change will effect their salary, status, security, sense of identity and self-esteem.

Step 1: Anticipate discomfort
Acknowledge that change is a transitionary period and that it will be accompanied by feelings of uncertainty and psychological discomfort. Don't brush these normal reactions aside – acknowledging the feelings that change can bring gives permission to actually feel these things and to air those feelings to others.

Step 2: Be positive
Try to be convinced or convince others of the benefits of the proposed change. Hamish (in the example above) didn't try hard enough to discover the benefits of email, but his manager failed too, by not explaining sufficiently the benefits of the system. Ultimately Hamish did not embrace the change because he did not believe in its value.

No one will accept change without knowing and believing in its advantages. Because change has such a bad press and is often associated with redundancies, many people will be suspicious.

The Employer and Change
You must – if in a position of superiority – be prepared to communicate effectively with your subordinates about the advantages of the proposed change.

One useful technique is to get your subordinates to convince each other that the change will have benefits, rather than you attempting to persuade them. If one person is won over, have them explain the advantages to everyone else. If no one other than yourself is won over, try splitting your group into two with one group trying to come up with convincing arguments to persuade the other. People are more likely to be convinced by their own peers, even if they know that those peers are Devil's Advocates.

The Employee and Change

"When our company was taken over by a much larger one I braced myself for the misery and hassle I expected. I was pleasantly surprised. I had thought that things had been fine as they were before the merger, but things really improved post-merger. Bureaucracy became more efficient, our expenses were paid on time, we had clear lines of supervision, clear complaints procedures and a management that really seemed to listen."

Elaine, Human Resources Assistant

As an employee, you should remain open-minded. Always be ready to see the positive effects of change, as Elaine did. Don't presume that everything will go badly.

Step 3: Plan ahead

Many people make the mistake of assuming that the changes will have no effect at all. If this were true, there would be little point in making the changes. Instead of ignoring the changes, then, acknowledge them by having – if you are a manager – one or more sessions in which your staff can voice their concerns. If you cannot answer their questions immediately, get back to them as soon as you can. Always be as honest as possible, but do try to stress the positive elements.

Step 4: Spread ownership

"I had been working in an office on the third floor of the building, when one day I received an email from my line-manager, informing me that I was to move to an eighth-floor office. I was furious – not that I was moving, but that I had not been consulted. I dug my heels in and made life very awkward for my manager. I told him that if he had asked me, I would have said yes, but the way he had foisted the move on me had really annoyed me. I wouldn't move until I had a whole list of demands met, like new furniture. He could have avoided all that hassle by just consulting me."

Nigel, Communications Officer

When people have some ownership or influence over the direction that the change is taking they will feel psychologically more powerful, thus happier.

If the change is being foisted upon you, try to gain ownership of a small part of it by negotiating with your manager: explain how you feel, and tell them how having input to the decisions and propositions would help you to see things in a more positive manner.

This will also help your manager – remember, whoever accepts the situation can become an ambassador for the change, spreading the positive message to more reluctant colleagues.

3. Leading

As your career advances you will inevitably become responsible for the supervision of other people. As soon as this happens, you are effectively a 'leader', and how you lead will greatly influence your success and career advancement from here. Whether you are a manager, supervisor, team captain, line manager or team leader, if you lead well your subordinates will be motivated and productive, and you will be seen as successful.

A Good Leader

What makes a good leader?

"A good leader should be able to motivate their workforce. I think that is the main characteristic they need."

"They should be able to inspire people to reach for heights they would never have reached alone. They should inspire people to work not just for the pay cheque, but because of a loyalty to the firm and the leader."

"A good leader should be fair and treat people well."

"They should be approachable, not distant. You should be able to discuss anything with a good leader."

"They should nurture their staff, not hold them back."

"A truly great leader is one who demands the best but who rewards you fairly."
From a survey that asked 'What makes a good leader?'

The qualities of leadership have probably been debated more than any other subject in this book. Some people argue that good leaders are charismatic, others that they are good motivators. Many approaches assume that you either are a good leader or you're not. In other words, leaders are born, not developed. Other people say that many leaderships skills can be learnt, and that many good leaders improved by learning how to lead.

What we can be sure of is that, because different styles of leadership may be required for different groups of people or for different situations, leadership skills are extremely difficult to define. Despite this the examples at the beginning of this section begin to create an image of the ideal leader as:

- motivating
- inspiring
- fair
- approachable
- nurturing
- demanding

Do You Have Potential?

You may or may not have all or some of the characteristics mentioned above. What is more important is that you have some basic potential to lead. Complete this Leadership Potential Scale by making a note, on a piece of paper, of the number indicating your agreement with each statement.

1: Agree strongly.
2: Agree.
3: Neither agree nor disagree.
4: Disagree.
5: Disagree strongly.

People consider me to be responsible.
I get on well with different people.
I enjoy social situations.
People (such as friends) often come to me with their problems.
I am good at persuading and influencing others.
I often take the lead naturally.
I accept that others may not always like me.
I can control my emotions at work.
I am very hard-working.
I believe communication is very important.
I am good at expressing my thoughts verbally.
I am always punctual.
I do not always need to win at everything I do.
I believe in being compassionate at work.
I think I could be tough if necessary.
I work well in teams.
I can admit if I have made a mistake.
I am able to delegate.
I am happy for others to achieve and gain recognition.
I am open to new ideas.

Less than 40

You already have a great deal of leadership potential – read on to find out how to really develop this potential.

Between 40 and 80

Those people who scored between 41 and 79 can choose either to rely on the information below, or to do some supplementary work. Leadership books provide very valuable advice, as do Leadership Development Courses.

Greater than 80

You do not, as yet, seem to have leadership potential. This does not mean that you will never make a good leader; simply that you are probably not yet ready to take a leadership role.

If you scored over 80 and are actually in a leadership role, don't panic. You can greatly improve your skills, using the following guidelines as a basis, and pursuing some further recommended reading.

The Skills You Will Need

Skills that will help you to become an effective leader include:

- communication

- delegation

- motivation

- taking initiative

- planning and goal-setting

- team-building

Communication

Possibly the most important element of communication, for anyone in a leadership position, is the ability to listen.

Most good managers are skilled communicators – they present their ideas clearly and can persuade others articulately – but a true leader must also be able to listen. This crucial skill will be required in many different situations, when the manager listens to subordinates' problems, concerns or ideas, superiors, groups, suppliers, angry customers... and so on.

How to listen

Good listening skills can be learned. Practice the five-step plan below, based on professional counselling skills:

Step 1: At first, keep quiet

Give the speaker time to talk: don't jump in, correct them, or finish their sentences. Speak only when you are sure that the other person has had every opportunity to say what they want to say.

Step 2: Then, reflect

Summarise or paraphrase the speaker's comments, preceding this with a comment along the lines of the following:

Example:

"Let me be clear that I have understood. You're saying that..."

or:

"Are you saying...?"

Step 3: Use your body
Use body language to convey empathy and understanding by:

- sitting with your body turned towards the other person.

- nodding periodically, but not too often.

- maintaining eye contact, but glancing away momentarily.

- not taking too many notes, or doodling on your notepad.

Step 4: Probe
Encourage the speaker to really open up. Gentle probing questions should always be open-ended, and include:
> **Example:**
> *"And what happened next...?"*
> *"How did that make you feel?"*
> *"What would you like to see happen?"*
> *"Can you tell me more?"*

Step 5: Use 'active listening'
'Active listening' is not the same as just keeping quiet, which many people assume is what a listener does. Active listening may be extremely responsive and techniques include:

- appearing to be paying attention by using the appropriate body language, and by varying your responses.

- listening to the whole sentence or speech – people often think about what they are going to say next and rarely hear the whole speech. This is one of the first things that counsellors are taught.

- reflecting.

- echoing – a reflection technique, which involves repeating the speaker's last couple of words.

- verifying and checking the facts, rather than the emotions being expressed.
  > **Example:**
  > **Speaker:** *"The other team members don't even turn up for meetings!"*
  > **Listener:** *"How many turned up for the last meeting?"*

- summarising.

- asking for examples – this can help the listener gain a full picture of the full situation.

- encouraging – with non-verbal signs such as nodding, or verbal agreements.

Delegation
Delegation is a crucial aspect of the leader's role – if no work is delegated to others, there is nothing to lead.

As one author puts it, 'In order to manage, it is necessary to manage the work of other people. This involves the process of delegation'. Here, delegation is defined as the process of 'Entrusting authority and responsibility to others'. [Source: Mullins, 1996]

Why delegate?
"I can do it quicker myself."
"I delegated once and the other person let me down."
"I can never decide which tasks to hand over."

Many people are reluctant to delegate, as the above examples show. For every argument against delegation, however, there is a more effective counter-argument:

Against	For
"I don't like having to ask my subordinates to do tasks – I feel as if I am passing on the tasks I don't want to do."	Others should know that your job as a leader is to delegate. If they don't know this, then explain it. Balance the work that you cannot do with challenging tasks that they want to do.
"I can do the tasks quicker than them – in fact, I can do them in the time it takes to explain what the task is!"	On the first occasion this is probably true, but they will soon learn, and perform the tasks quickly. Part of your role as a leader is to develop your subordinates' skills, and they can't do this if you don't let them perform new tasks.
"I feel in less control if other people are doing my work."	Firstly, you shouldn't see any work as exclusively 'mine'. In addition, control can be maintained by asking for regular updates and feedback. You should eventually learn to reduce the amount of control you need.
"If they make a mistake it is my responsibility."	Part of being able to manage is allowing others to make mistakes. Keep tabs on them, but accept the risk involved as part of the learning experience for you and your staff.

The important thing is to know when, how and how much to delegate to others. The following six-step plan should prove useful to those who are confused about delegation matters.

Step 1: Identify the tasks
Decide which tasks you think could be delegated: those which are within the capabilities of other people; those which will provide others with vital training experiences; or those which you simply do not have the time to do yourself.

Step 2: Write down the tasks
Make a written note of what needs to be done and when. It is always good to clarify your requests in written form, allowing less room for misunderstandings.

Step 3: Talk about the tasks
Ask the person who is going to do the work how they might best carry it out. Allowing them the initiative to work to their own methods is better than trying to enforce your own system of working and will empower your subordinate.

Step 4: Get reports on the tasks
Agree on how and when you will be updated on progress. You might, for instance, agree to receive a weekly update or a daily email. It is better to agree this in advance than to start pestering the other person regularly for feedback.

Step 5: Relinquish ownership of the tasks
Give the delegate ownership by letting them be responsible for the work, and allowing them to take the credit – or otherwise – for it. This is an important managerial skill: people work more effectively on those tasks for which they feel responsible.

Step 6: Stay on hand
Finally, be there to offer advice, support and encouragement. Don't just dump the work and run.

It has been assumed so far that you will be delegating purely to subordinates; however, it is also possible that you will at some point be delegating to, or leading, your own peers. In a team, for example, some group members often take on leadership roles for particular projects. Nevertheless, exactly the same principles apply in all situations.

Motivation
"The money offered for this job is half as much as that which I could get in management, which I've been trained in. I could probably get a job paying much more – in fact I've been in jobs that pay much more. But at the end of the day I realised that money wasn't everything. There are other things that motivate me to get out of bed and into work every day. For me, these things were job satisfaction, and a feeling that I was doing something useful and valuable. I want to give something to society, not just earn a whole wad of money."
Ben, Trainee Physiotherapist

Motivation is the driving force that explains peoples' choice of one particular course of action in preference to another; the force which keeps them going even in the face of difficulties and problems. **[Source: Krech, Crutchfield and Ballachey, 1962]** Trying to keep employees or subordinates motivated over time is one of the greatest challenges for a leader. A good manager or leader must be able to identify the individual motivators within a team – and then endeavour to use these factors to motivate the members.

Are you a motivator?
To find out how effective you are at motivating, ask yourself the following questions.

Do you know what motivates your workers?

Have you ever asked them what they are motivated by?

The last time they achieved something, did you congratulate them directly in any way?

Do they generally make their own decisions?

Do you hold regular reviews with them?

So, what motivates?
Money or financial reward is a great motivator, but by no means the only one. In fact, people will often work for less money in jobs where other motivating factors exist. [Source: Hertzberg, 1966]

Recognition
Good leaders do not claim credit for things that their subordinates have achieved. Great leaders set their subordinates up for recognition; in other words, they look for ways in which their subordinates can gain credit for their own successes. This could involve allowing people the opportunity to present their work to senior management, or at a conference.

Some managers award buttons or pins, medals or certificates to acknowledge individuals' successes. Others publicise their subordinates' work within the organisation's newsletters, and sometimes in the local press.

Insecure leaders should remember that any credit or recognition given to members of their team automatically reflects well on them.

Achievement
Most people are motivated by a sense of achievement, by bringing something to a successful conclusion, completing a job or solving a problem. The sense of achievement will be maximised if individuals are given ownership of their tasks, and thus feel that the tasks are being performed for themselves as well as for a leader.

Status
The degree to which some people are motivated by status is quite amazing.

Such people choose their cars, decorate their homes, select holiday destinations and even clothe themselves in status-enhancing ways. At work, status is sought through job titles, office size, office furniture, car park spaces and other perks.

There are, however, more discreet ways to enhance the status of deserving employees: by, for example, inviting them to meet important visitors or by asking their opinion or advice on important matters.

Responsibility
"I left my last job because of the lack of responsibility. I worked as a store assistant, but I wanted to learn skills like till operation, stock-taking, etc. I wasn't allowed, because I hadn't been in the post one year. I found this so frustrating and felt like I

was stupid, or not to be trusted. Worse still was the fact that we had to consult our line manager over every little customer query – even things like them paying by cheque or credit card, or returning something to the store. The customers got fed up with waiting while we consulted our boss. And I found it all so de-motivating."

Ava, Sales Assistant

Most people are motivated by being able to make decisions and by being trusted. Without such empowerment, people may well feel de-motivated.

A good leader will also recognise that different people are motivated by different things. Unlike Ava, some people are quite happy not to have any responsibility. They simply require the kind of job where they don't have to think or worry.

Interest

Any job must have some intrinsic appeal in order for it to be motivating. People will become bored by repetitive or monotonous tasks, or by work that seems pointless. Explaining to workers why a task needs doing, rather than just insisting that it is done, will create motivation and interest. Additionally, a good leader will maintain job interest by matching the skills and abilities of the workers with those of the job.

'Higher order altruism'

This describes the motivation created by working for the greater good rather than for personal or material gain. Thus some people will work in low-paid jobs that involve helping others, rather than in well-paid ones that help only themselves.

Taking Initiative

Leaders must have the confidence to initiate projects and tasks, and to take the initiative generally, while knowing when to let their subordinates take the initiative.

In taking the initiative, you must be decisive and at all times retain the courage of your convictions. You should also be capable of quickly assessing risk, and prepared to take a risk when necessary.

To take the initiative, follow the five-step plan below.

Step 1: Look out for good ideas

Always be thinking about how things can be improved. Question everything. This will create an initiative-taking mindset, making you open to new ideas and ready to question the status quo.

Step 2: Be objective

It is easy to get excited about a new concept or idea, but 90 per cent of these will be useless. Taking initiative is not about running with every idea that falls into your lap, but about being selective. Decide which ones might be worth pursuing by doing some research: read up on related ideas (also use the internet, or CD-ROMs), and ask colleagues or subordinates what they think.

Step 3: Trust your instinct

"A publisher had approached me and sent me a contract for a book. On paper they sounded ideal and I thought they could offer me everything I wanted. But I kept delaying signing the contract, and wasn't sure why. One night, it hit me. I listened to my instinct and it was telling me that this publisher wasn't right for me. I couldn't put my finger on why not, but once I made the decision to find another publisher, I felt happier. I don't know if I made the right choice or not, but a colleague of mine who has written a book for the same publisher has since told me how unhappy with them he is."

Richard, Author

For those who need to use their initiative, a good and trustworthy instinct or 'sixth sense' is vital. Many great leaders have gone with an idea, even in the face of logical opposition, because gut instinct said, 'Go for it'.

Develop and learn to trust your instinct by listening to it. When a decision needs to be made, pay some attention to that inner voice.

Step 4: Enthuse!

Once you have decided to take the initiative, proceed with boundless enthusiasm. Enthusiasm rubs off on others and makes the difference between taking the initiative and carrying out another task.

Step 5: Accept the worst

You may have to face the fact that some initiatives fail. It happens. Nothing is fool-proof.

> **Golden Rule**
> A good leader is always open to new initiatives.

Planning and Goal-Setting

A university department faced closure due to lack of funding and interest in its courses. The head of the department, Tony, used planning and goal-setting to come up with an action plan. He takes up the story:

"I realised that we only had funding for another 18 months, so my objective was very clear and specific – we had somehow to raise enough money to make us financially viable for at least three years. I knew that we had really just one year in which to do that. With that objective in mind, I got together with my eight-strong team, and we brainstormed ideas about how we could reach our objective. We came up with several good ideas, including introducing new courses to bring students in, applying to research bodies for funding money and running a residential course for managers. That was three approaches and we divided them up and allocated members of the team to each one. Within each of the three strategies, detailed action plans were devised outlining how exactly we could go about each task and what would be involved. Everything was written down, and each stage of each plan was agreed by all involved.

"The next task was to work out how much time would be needed to put each plan into practice. It was January when we started and we reckoned it would take six months to set up our residential course, as that involved finding location, planning a and preparing the course, advertising for recruits, and so on. The funding applications involved finding institutions to apply to, studying the literature in order to devise projects to carry out, and writing the applications. That, we thought, would involve two to eight months and could be a rolling plan. The new course would have to be started in the new academic year – October – so our timescale was fixed for that.

"Having done all that, every single tiny task was broken down according to when it needed to be done by. Then we all got on and did it. Unfortunately, a problem arose when one key member of the team left to work elsewhere. All her tasks had to be divided out again amongst the rest of the team and we had to amend our objectives with regards to the course contents, to reflect the loss of her input."

Tony's well-thought-out plan worked, and within a year new income was being generated.

Every astute worker needs to be able to plan and set goals for themselves. A leader, however, must be able to do this for other people, for groups and for the company as a whole.

Are you a planner?
Some people are born planners, others need training.

If you are a natural planner and goal-setter you will be able to answer 'yes' to the following questions:

Do I know how my working day will be filled for the next four weeks?

Do I have a vision about how I see my career work-wise, a year from now?

Am I proactive in making things happen?

Am I constantly looking for new challenges?

Am I doing things that will only benefit me much later?

How to plan
Like Tony, at the beginning of this section, you need to know the four main steps of planning and goal-setting.

Step 1: Decide your objectives
The manager of a high street clothes shop, Sally, has an objective to make her sales branch 'the best'.

The goals that you set must be specific and obtainable. Sally's goal is not sufficiently specific; she would be advised to define more closely her concept of 'the best'.

Sally writes:
Best means: the most sales; fewest complaints; lowest absenteeism; lowest job turnover.

This is better, but still not very obtainable at this point.

Sally amended her goals:
- to increase the sales figures to higher than average.
- to reduce customer complaints to lower than average.
- to reduce absenteeism of her team by 50 per cent.
- to reduce the number of staff who leave their job in her branch by 50 per cent.

Step 2: Decide your plan
The next step is to work out how you will achieve these objectives. At this stage, the best strategy is to hold a 'brainstorm': engage your whole team, and write down various ideas for ways of meeting each objective.

Sally and her team came up with these strategies:

Goal 1: Increase sales figures by:	Goal 2: Reduce customer complaints by:
• improving displays. • attending courses on window display, or getting someone in to do the windows. • improving the sales techniques of sales advisors. • attending sales courses at head office. • introducing a commission scheme.	• improving customer service. • attending customer service courses. • offering a no-quibble money-back guarantee. • smiling and being polite. • having a customer care policy.
Goal 3: Reduce absenteeism by:	**Goal 4: Reduce staff turnover by:**
• having a reward system for no absences. • making work more interesting. • having a sales commission. • providing stress counselling.	• finding out why people leave. • having exit questionnaires. • introducing a suggestions box. • having better promotion prospects.

Step 3: Decide on a timescale
Not every strategy can be implemented immediately. It is probably a good idea to establish a timescale for the plans: perhaps working to a one-year time-frame for some of them, and putting others in motion for completion the following year.

It is important to be realistic, and to remember that seeking advice, permission and funds inevitably takes longer than one expects.

Step 4: Review everything
Everything changes: a good leader will not set a plan rolling without constant review and re-examination. After an agreed time it must be decided whether or not the objectives are being reached, if the same goals still apply, and if those performing the tasks are performing them adequately.

Team-building

SEE CHAPTER 4

For a new leader presented with a disparate group of individuals who have separate interests and who need to work together, the first step is to build a team.

In reality, team-building is simply an attempt by a facilitator to take people quickly and formally through the group development stages described in Chapter Four. A team-builder needs to establish:

* a shared set of aims with an agreed strategy for achieving them.

* a team leader who facilitates this process.

* co-operation and shared support.

* some shared tasks, but clearly defined roles.

* an emotional bond which holds the team together.

How to build a team

Step 1: Carefully form your group
Ensure that it has:

* the correct number of people (at least three, and probably no more than eight or ten).

* regular meetings and interactions.

* stable memberships – that people are not continually leaving, with new members joining.

* the correct mix of required skills and experiences.

* adequate resources and support from the organisation.

Step 2: Ensure that there are goals and roles
"We were there with the specific aim of finding a new market for our product. The aim of the team was clear, but I was not sure what I could do myself. I am a designer, and my job is to design whatever I am asked to design. It is not my job to sell or find markets – I wouldn't know where to start. I had been asked to join the team, but I really couldn't see how I could contribute, so I quit after a while – I felt I could use my time in better ways."

Nadine, Designer

Team-members must know firstly the goals of the team and equally importantly, how to contribute to these goals. As Nadine discovered, many teams fail because members are not clear about their goals, or are unsure about how to help the group achieve them.

A good team-builder clarifies both the group aims and the roles each member will take. Ask each member how they see their role and in what ways they think their own skills contribute towards the group goals.

Step 3: Norming

 SEE CHAPTER | 4

A group naturally passes through this stage, but a leader will help members through it more quickly. Techniques for speeding-up the norming stage include:

- suggesting ground-rules, rights and responsibilities yourself.

- using brainstorming so that each member suggests their own ideas.

- ensuring that each member accepts all the rules.

Step 4: Storming

 SEE CHAPTER | 4

Even the most well-built teams will go through a 'storming' phase. Problems will arise, and those which typically confront the team-builder include:

Too-rapid progress
Many teams fail when a team goes straight to the Performing stage, if the leader has not spent sufficient time building it properly. If the other three stages are not dealt with, many ground-rules will not be established, and some members will not even know what their task is.

No bond between members
Again this is a symptom of poor team development. Team-building exercises will help to build a cohesive bond. Such exercises involve artificial situations where members have to work together on a task. Some exercises take an hour, some an afternoon, others an entire day – but all will strengthen relationships and draw out the potential of other team members.

Example:
Ice-breaking exercises
Examples include 'Human Bingo'. Every member is given a grid of 12 squares. In each square is a description of a person who has, for example, one cat, three sisters, who has been to Australia, appeared on television, and so on. The task is for the members to match all the people in the group with the descriptions in the squares, with the winner being the first to match all 12.

Problem solving exercises
It doesn't matter too much what the problem is – the important thing is that the team is able to work together to find a solution.

Physical tasks
Examples include building a bridge out of chairs or tables that will allow every team member to cross – within a time limit. Such tasks should allow different people to contribute in different ways, and should develop a team bond.

Group reliance tasks
Every member is reliant on everyone else. Examples include asking a team

to imagine that they are a paper aeroplane manufacturer, and their task is to produce as many identical planes as possible. The team should quickly realise that the only way to do this is to set up a kind of production line, whereby each member performs the same task in the same way. For instance, A folds the paper once, B executes the second fold, C makes the 'nose' of the plane and D colours the tail-wing.

Competition exercises
One psychological technique that can be used to build a team bond involves having some sort of competition with another group or team. The opposition can be from another company, or within the same company, and the competition can be about anything at all, as long as people want to win.

Step 5: Evaluate and control the team
The goal of a team-leader is to facilitate the team's performances, rather than simply to give orders to its members. As facilitator, you must ensure that everyone has a chance to participate, that everyone's views are heard, that the task does not become more important than the process – but equally that the process does not overshadow the task.

Chapter Checkpoint

After reading this chapter, you should:

- know how to plan your career.

- have learnt how to manage, and cope with, change.

- know what makes a good leader and how to become one yourself.

Further Reading

Peel, M., *Career Development and Planning: A Guide for Managers, Trainers and Personnel* (New York: McGraw-Hill, 1992).

Adair, J., *Leadership Skills* (London: Institute of Personnel and Development, 1992).

Clemmer, J., *Leadership for Every Manager* (London: Piatkus, 1989).

Coates, J., and C. Breeze, *Delegating with Confidence* (London: Institute of Personnel and Development, 1996).

Wilson, T., *A Manual for Change* (Aldershot: Gower Publishing, 1994).

Conclusion

If you have learnt only one lesson from this book, that lesson should be that it is no longer sufficient just to do your job well.

The really important work skills for the twenty-first century are not taught in schools, colleges or universities. Where are the qualifications in communication skills? The degrees in teamwork? The diplomas in getting on with people? Where are the Masters programmes in organisational politics? The examinations in ability to motivate?

The major preoccupation of society today is with qualifications in everything... except in those transferable skills that really count.

There are school-leavers who cannot pick up the phone and ask a potential employer about a job vacancy.

There are university graduates who do not know how to work in a team.

There are people in top management who have no idea how to motivate their staff, how to spread ownership of change, or how to empower their workers.

There are millions of middle-management and junior-level workers who ignore office politics, hoping that they will go away; who avoid being assertive in the hope of leading a quiet life; who do not know how to behave at the office party, or what to wear for a working lunch.

These basic, transferable skills should be part of every school's curriculum, part of every college and university's agenda, and an integral feature of every organisation's induction or training schemes.

But they are not; hence the need for *Psychology Goes to Work*. By reading this book, you have given yourself the sustainable competitive advantage needed to survive and succeed in the turbulent modern world of work.

Regardless of the level at which you now find yourself, by allowing psychology to accompany you to work, you will achieve an extra edge in the workplace.

You can now:

- manage your Personal PR.

- identify the hidden codes and rules of the office environment.

- get on with even the most difficult colleagues, bosses, customers or subordinates.

- work successfully in a team, and help other team members to achieve their full potential.

- profit from the tricky areas of gossip, politics and power.

- communicate properly.

- handle your stress more effectively.

- be more assertive.

- learn to be a more effective leader.

All these are the real skills that will take you to the top.
The skills you should never be without.
The skills that you take with you when *Psychology Goes to Work.*

Bibliography

Albrecht, K., *Stress and the Manager: Making It Work for You* (New Jersey: Prentice-Hall, 1979).

Arnold, J., C. L. Cooper, and **I. T. Robertson,** *Work Psychology: Understanding Human Behaviour in the Workplace* (London: Financial Times Pitman Publishing, 1998).

Asch, S. E., 'Opinions and Social Pressure', *Scientific American*, 193, no. 5 (1955), 31–35.

Baron, R. A., *Behavior in Organizations* (Boston: Allyn and Bacon, 1986), p.223.

Belbin, R. M., *Management Teams: Why They Succeed or Fail* (London: Heinemann, 1981).

Belbin, R. M., *Team Roles at Work: A Strategy for Human Resource Management* (Oxford: Butterworth-Heinemann, 1993).

Birdwhistell, R. L., *Kinesics and Context* (Philadelphia: University of Pennsylvania Press, 1970).

Cannon, W. B., *The Wisdom of the Body* (New York: Norton, 1939).

Cattell, R. B., *Intelligence: Its Structure, Growth and Action* (New York: Elsevier Science, 1987).

Cattell, R. B., H. W. Eber, and **M. M. Taksuoka,** *Handbook for the Sixteen Personality Factor Questionnaire* (Windsor: National Foundation for Educational Research, 1970).

Costa, P. T., and **R. R. McCrae,** *The NEO PI-R Professional Manual* (Odessa: Psychological Assessment Resources Inc., 1992).

Dance, F. E. X., and **C. E. Larson,** *The Functions of Human Communication: A Theoretical Approach* (New York: Holt, Rinehart & Winston, 1976).

Davis, M., E. E. Robbins, and **M. McKay,** *The Relaxation and Stress Reduction Workbook* (New York: MJF Books, 1995).

Deutsch, M., and **H. B. Gerrard,** 'A Study of Normative and Informational Social Influences upon Individual Judgement', *Journal of Abnormal and Social Psychology*, 51 (1955), 629–36.

Di Martino, V., and **L. Wirth,** 'Telework: A New Way of Working and Living', *International Labour Review*, 129, no. 5 (1990).

Eysenck, H. J., and **S. B. G. Eysenck,** *Manual of the Eysenck Personality Scales* (London: Hodder and Stoughton, 1991).

Ezzamel, M., C. Green, S. Lilley, and **H. Willmott,** 'Change Management: Appendix 1-A, Review and Analysis of Recent Changes in UK Management Practices' (Manchester: The Financial Services Research Centre, UMIST, 1994).

Falkenberg, L. E., 'Employee Fitness Programmes: Their Impact on the Employee and the Organization', *Academy of Management Review*, 12, no. 3 (1987), 511–22.

Fisher, D., *Communication in Organizations* (Minnesota: West Publishing Company, 1993).

Forbes, R. J., and **P. R. Jackson,** 'Non-Verbal Behavior and the Outcomes of Selection Interviews', *Journal of Occupational Psychology*, 53 (1980), 65–72.

Friedman, M., and **R. H. Rosenman,** *Type A Behaviour and Your Heart* (London: Wildwood House, 1974).

Galinsky, E., J. T. Bond, and **D. E. Friedman,** *The Changing Workforce: Highlights of the National Study* (New York: Families and Work Institute, 1993).

Goffman, E., *The Presentation of Self in Everyday Life* (Garden City, New York: Doubleday, 1959).

Goleman, D., *Emotional Intelligence: Why It Can Matter More Than IQ* (London: Bloomsbury Publishing, 1996), p.115.

Hall, E., *The Silent Language* (Greenwich, Connecticut: Fawcett, 1959).

Handy, C., *The Empty Raincoat* (London: Hutchinson, 1994).

Hartley, R. F., *Marketing Mistakes* (New York: John Wiley, 1992).

Hatfield, E., J. Cacioppo, and **R. L. Rapson,** 'Primitive Emotional Contagion', in *Review of Personality and Social Psychology*, ed. by M. S. Clark (California: Sage, 1992), XIV, 151–177.

Hellriegel, D., J. W. Slocum, and **R. W. Woodman,** *Organizational Behavior* (Missouri: West, 1989), p.37.

Hertzberg, F., *Work and the Nature of Man* (Cleveland, Ohio: World Publishing, 1966).

Hill, E. J., A. J. Hawkins, and **B. C. Miller,** 'Work and Family in the Virtual Office', *Family Relations*, 45, no. 3 (1996).

Hochschild, A., *The Managed Heart: Commercialization of Human Feeling* (Berkeley: University of California Press, 1983).

Holland, J. L., *The Self-Directed Search: Professional Manual* (Odessa: Psychological Assessment Resources Inc., 1985).

House, R. J., and **M. L. Baetz,** 'Leadership: Some Empirical Generalizations and New Research Directions', in *Research in Organizational Behavior*, ed. by L. L. Cummings and B. M. Staw (Greenwich, Connecticut: JAI Press, 1979), I.

Huws, U., 'The New Homeworkers: New Technology and the Changing Location of White-Collar Work', *Low Pay Pamphlet*, 28 (London, Low Pay Unit, 1984).

Janis, I. L., *Victims of Groupthink* (Boston: Houghton Mifflin, 1972).

Jung, C., *The Psychology of the Transference* (Princeton, New Jersey: Princeton University Press, 1974).

Kornhauser, A., *Mental Health of the Industrial Worker* (New York: John Wiley, 1965).

Krech, D., R. S. Crutchfield, and **E. Ballachey,** *Individual in Society* (Singapore: McGraw-Hill, 1962).

Luthans, F., *Organizational Behavior* (Singapore: McGraw-Hill, 1992).

Mann, S., and **R. Jones,** 'The Expression and Suppression of Emotion in Intra-organisational Communications'. Paper presented at the Annual Conference of the British Psychology Society Division of Occupational Psychology, Blackpool, January 1997.

Mann, S., 'Politics and Power in Organizations: Why Women Lose Out', *Leadership and Organizational Development Journal*, 16, no. 2 (1995), 9–15.

Mann, S., 'Achieving Corporate Communication Excellence: the Cost to Health', *Book of Proceedings of the Tenth Conference on Corporate Communications*, New Jersey, 1997.

Matteson, M. T., and **J. M. Ivancevich,** 'Individual Stress Management Interventions: Evaluation of Techniques', *Journal of Managerial Psychology*, 2, no. 1 (1987) 24–30.

McCrae, R. R., and **P. T. Costa,** *Personality in Adulthood* (New York: Guildford, 1990).

Mehrabian, A., *Tactics of Social Influence* (New Jersey: Prentice-Hall, 1970).

Morgan, G., *Images of Organizations* (London: Sage, 1986).

Moscovici, S., *Social Influence and Social Change* (London: Academic Press, 1976).

Mullins, L. J., *Management and Organisational Behaviour* (London: Pitman Publishing, 1996).

Nilles, J. M., *Making Telecommuting Happen: A Guide for Telemanagers and Telecommuters* (New York: van Nostrand Reinhold, 1994).

Occupational Personality Questionnaire Manual (Surrey: Saville and Holdsworth Ltd., 1990).

Pratt, J. M., 'Home Teleworking: A Study of its Pioneers', *Technological Forecasting and Social Change*, 25, no. 1 (1984).

Rafaeli, A., and **R. I. Sutton,** 'The Expression of Emotion in Organizational Life', in Cummings and Staw, XI, 1–42.

Rosenfeld, P., R. A. Giacalone, and **C. A. Riordan,** *Impression Management in Organizations* (London: Routledge, 1995).

Rotter, J. B., 'Generalized Expectancies for Internal versus External Locus of Control of Reinforcement', *Psychological Monographs*, 30, no. 1 (1966),1–26.

Selye, H., 'The General Adaptation Syndrome and the Diseases of Adaptation', *Journal of Clinical Endocrinology*, no. 6 (1946), 117.

Selye, H., *Stress Without Distress* (Philadelphia: J. B. Lippincott, 1974).

Settoon, R. P., N. Bennett, and **R. C. Liden,** 'Social Exchange in Organizations: Perceived Organizational Support, Leader-Member Exchange and Employee Reciprocity', *Journal of Applied Psychology*, 81, no. 3 (1996), 219–227.

Snyder, M., *Public Appearances/Private Realities: the Psychology of Self-Monitoring* (New York: W. H. Freeman, 1986).

Spingbett, B. M., 'Factors Affecting the Final Decision in the Employment Interview', *Canadian Journal of Psychology*, 111 (1958) 42–61.

Sutherland, V. J., and **C. L. Cooper,** *Understanding Stress: A Psychological Perspective for Health Professionals* (Suffolk: Chapman & Hall, 1993).

Tisdelle, D. A., D. J. Hansen, J. S. St Lawrence, and **J. C. Brown,** 'Stress Management Training for Dental Students', *Journal of Dental Education*, 48, (1984), 196–201.

Tuckman, B. W., 'Development Sequence in Small Groups', *Psychological Bulletin,* 63, (1965), 284–499.

Turner, J., 'Will Telecommuting Ever Get Off the Ground?', *Sternbusiness Magazine*, Summer 1998.

Van Maanen, J., and **G. Kunda,** 'Real Feelings: Emotional Expression and Organizational Culture', in Cummings and Staw, XI, 343–103.

Walker-Burt, G., *Relationships Between Person-Environment Fit, Psychological Strain and Coping Behaviors Among Student Nurses* (Ann Arbor, Michigan: University Microfilms International, 1980).

Wallechinsky, D., and **I. Wallace,** *The Book of Lists* (William Morrow: New York, 1977).

Walton, E., 'How Efficient is the Grapevine?', *Personnel*, March-April (1961), 45–49.

Wardwell, W., I. M. Hyman, and **C. B. Bahnson,** 'Stress and Coronary Disease in Three Field Studies', *Journal of Chronic Disease*, no. 17 (1964), 73–4.

Wheatley, M., *The Future of Middle Management* (London: British Institute of Management, 1992).

Wilkes, R. B., M. N. Frolick, and **R. Urwiler,** 'Critical Issues in Developing Successful Telework Programs', *Journal of Systems Management*, 45, no. 7 (1994).

Copyright Notice

Index